Visions of the Future:
HR Strategies for the New Millennium

Marc G. Singer
Editor

PREFACE

Much has been written about the need for human resources practitioners to become strategic partners in their organizations. The most important elements of strategic planning are the ability to identify emerging trends and understand how these trends will affect the way we do our business.

We are extraordinarily grateful for the wealth of talent found in the membership of the Society for Human Resource Management's national committees. These professionals have looked ahead, and in their own area of expertise they are presenting to us likely scenarios for the near future. Under the guidance of Dr. Marc G. Singer, past SHRM Research Committee Chair, and with invaluable assistance from SHRM staff, SHRM's committees selected the issues most likely to have the highest impact on the field of human resource management in the next century. The main purpose of this book is to cause the reader to become ever vigilant for change in the environment and how this change will impact human resources. How quickly we identify the trends, and how ready we are to respond to them, will determine to a great degree how credible and successful we are in our respective organizations.

Here, then, is the collective effort of many professionals. Enjoy and utilize the insights offered to make your world the envy of all around you. Our wish is that this book will influence you to become future-focused.

Michael J. Lotito, SPHR
Chair 2000

Ommy Strauch, SPHR
Vice President for Committees 1999–2000

ACKNOWLEDGMENTS

Predicting the future of Human Resources is at best a risky business. Academicians, practitioners, and researchers offer varying opinions about the issues that will have the greatest impact on human resource managers over the next decade. HR writings abound in areas such as government rules and regulations, the future role of unions, core competencies, costing HR, measurement, accountability, changing workforce demographics, and global impacts. The single constant that underlies these various perspectives appears to be the probability that the role of human resource management will undergo a significant transformation in the near future.

In an effort to identify some of the key issues facing the human resource profession during the early years of the millennium, professional volunteer members of SHRM's functional committees combined their numerous talents and energies. The result of this synergy is this book, *Visions of the Future: HR Strategies for the New Millennium*. I am especially grateful to Michael Lotito, SHRM Chair, whose leadership and support during the initial stages of the book enabled the commencement of this project, and to Ommy Strauch, Vice President for Committees, for her continuing assistance and encouragement during the project's completion phase. I am extremely thankful to the 1998 and 1999 SHRM committee chairs for their assistance in coordinating the efforts of their committees and for diligently monitoring their authors' contributions. I extend my thanks to the staff at SHRM who edited, formatted, and produced the final version of this project. Finally, I extend a special thank you to the members of the various committees and the authors for their time and efforts in writing this book.

Marc G. Singer
Editor
March 2000

ACKNOWLEDGMENTS

TABLE OF CONTENTS

Visions of the Future:
HR Strategies for the New Millennium

COMING OF AGE

Michael R. Losey
Society for Human Resource Management

The human resource management profession will profoundly change in the next century, as the United States and other developed countries evolve from manufacturing and service-based economies to knowledge-based ones. The industrial revolution created the human resource profession, and the twenty-first century workplace will require it to continue to transform itself. In the new millennium, human resource professionals must be fully accepted strategic business partners, leading their organizations through yet unidentified challenges in a rapidly changing global workplace. They will need to be more proactive in the design and implementation of workplace practices that will attract, retain, and motivate a shrinking pool of qualified workers.

In taking on that role, human resource professionals are now compelled to learn new skills that go beyond complex administration or being "gatekeepers." Their primary responsibilities have been to ensure compliance with labor contracts and federal and state laws, and to administer company policies and practices. In the twenty-first century, human resource professionals will be required to anticipate the needs of an increasingly white-collar workforce and plan strategically to meet those needs.

The trend is already happening. Companies are now realizing that the human resource function has a direct impact on their bottom lines and must be linked to core business strategies. Now, more than ever before, CEOs are asking, "Who is running this part of our company? Is that person competent?" There is a growing recognition that bona fide human resource professionals must understand economic, political, social, cultural, and demographic trends. They must also master technological innovations, changing work values, skill shortages, and global trends and practices, as well as government mandates in labor laws, affirmative action, health care, and privacy—to mention but a few areas of required competency. And, increasingly, human resource professionals must understand the business of business. Each day, the number of workplace issues in which human resource professionals must play a role increases, and their involvement in senior-level decision-making has become central to many organizations.

Yes, the human resource profession is now coming of age. In the new millennium, the profession will not require human resource professionals but human resource *leaders*. Higher levels of competencies will be required. The result will be higher barriers of entrance to the profession—as it should be in any demanding profession.

The H in HR—for History

To understand the future of the human resource profession, it is important to understand it through the lens of its history. It is a brief history, because the profession did not truly exist until the late nineteenth and early twentieth centuries, when the industrial revolution was at its peak.

Before the industrial revolution and the onset of mass production, there was little need for a profession dedicated to managing a workforce. As many as 90 percent of the people working in the United States were farmers. The remaining workers were tradesmen and craftsmen in business for themselves. There was no discussion about what the children would grow up to be. Farmers' sons knew what they would grow up to be: farmers. Daughters would become wives and mothers and care for the home. And they all learned their skills through their families.

Those vying to enter a trade were usually required to complete an extensive apprenticeship program under the tutelage of a master tradesman. These working relationships were close, personal relationships that rarely needed the intervention of a third party. Skilled craftsmen and apprentices worked in small shops or at home. There was little need for unions, workers' compensation, or labor laws on the family farm or in the small craft shop because workplace issues could be addressed through these personal relationships.

The industrial revolution, however, changed the nature of work. Now, through the application of electricity and other power sources, standardization of parts and tools, and improvements in processes, mass production was possible. For the first time, business owners could employ many workers in one location. Companies that designed a better product at less cost could use the railroad for efficiently shipping mass quantities of goods to previously out-of-reach markets, driving the demand for more goods and more workers. To feed that demand, immigration into the United States rose to an all-time high, and the most diverse workforce in the world began to take shape.

Unfortunately, though, abuses to workers were also at an all-time high. Labor laws such as minimum wage rate protection, overtime, workers' compensation, health and safety, or equal employment opportunity did not exist. Employers had little interest in their workers' personal lives, working conditions, or job satisfaction. Many companies were family-owned or dominated by one individual who believed that the employees' lots had improved through their employment. Any attempts to suggest changes were viewed as a threat to the owner's financial and personal interests. Many employers considered low-skilled employees in a mass production work environment as expendable.

Henry Ford allegedly commented that he didn't know why his employees insisted on bringing their heads to work when all he needed was their hands and feet. Ford's 380 percent turnover rate in 1913, which essentially crippled his company's ability to grow in an emerging industry, was a direct result of his attitude toward line workers and was driven by working conditions that were unacceptable at any wage. He agreed to double the workers' daily wage rate to five dollars so that he could stem turnover and buy employee loyalty, not so that "his workers could buy his cars" as some have suggested.

In many companies like the Ford Motor Company, the personnel people who previously had been given the largely administrative job of hiring low-wage, unskilled employees now saw that the well-being of employees had become much more important than how much they were paid. This became especially apparent as unions became more of a force to reckon with and as the nation's state and federal laws began to provide added protections to the interests of organized labor.

Many employers viewed the growing "union threat" as socialistic or radical, rather than as a self-preserving interest of workers in banding together to demand safer working conditions, humane treatment, and fair wages. And before the prohibition of unfair labor practices as we know them today, anti-union efforts were sometimes ruthlessly led by personnel representatives, some with security or police backgrounds. Industry viewed unions as its biggest and most powerful competitors because a union could shut down the employer faster or possibly disadvantage it more than any business competitor. This reality became a very real risk, and with risk comes interest and attention. The human resource profession became more important, and for the first time it mattered who was in the personnel job.

This was the environment that led to the rise of the modern union in the United States and, shortly thereafter, the human resource management profession. Unions rallied workers together to demand safer working conditions, humane treatment, and fair wages. They quickly became a force to be reckoned with, and while the political, social, and economic balance of power has shifted over time between unions and employer, unions have left an indelible mark on the American workplace.

The National Labor Relations Act, the Fair Labor Standards Act, the Taft-Hartley Act, the Equal Pay Act, the 1964 Civil Rights Act, the Age Discrimination in Employment Act, ERISA, the EOAA, OSHA, COBRA, the Americans with Disabilities Act, the Family and Medical Leave Act, and the Older Workers Protection Act, among others, have all been enacted, either directly or indirectly, because of the presence of the modern union in the American workplace.

Ironically, it is the passage of these laws that has aided in the steady decline of union membership since the mid-1950s. Today, only about 14 percent of the U.S. workforce is unionized, whereas in the late 1940s through the mid-1950s, one out of three workers were union members. These laws expanded protections to all workers, yet to some extent also usurped unions' roles in protecting workers. These legislative protections, along with the changing nature of the workforce, have dramatically affected the human resource profession.

Today, we are witnessing a historic social and economic shift into a knowledge-based economy, where we certainly want the employees to bring their heads to work. Today, it is not how many good parts you can make in an hour; it is how many good decisions you can make. Today, intellectual capital and the individual can make the crucial difference to an organization's success or failure.

The Future

What will all of this mean to the future of the workplace and the human resource profession?

Some may argue that the labor movement has become a dinosaur that will not last far into the next millennium. Falling membership rolls, the existence of federal labor laws that protect workers, and a growing white-collar workforce suggest that unions will become obsolete in the workplace of the twenty-first century.

My advice—don't count the unions out. A revitalization of the labor movement is taking place. We will see its survival through the increased unionization of white-collar and service-sector employees. Just this past year, physicians, who have a long-standing conservative outlook, voted to unionize to counter the powerful grip of health maintenance organizations on their fees and their practices. Temporary employees at Microsoft have also made moves to form a union. And the labor movement has moved to college campuses. At Stanford University, highly educated graduate assistants recently voted to join a union. At Dartmouth, undergraduates have focused their attention on fighting for a living wage for unskilled workers.

Yes, there will be a labor movement in the new millennium. But an increasing number of tomorrow's unions will consist of highly educated white-collar workers with very specific work skills. They will not look like or act like the old blue-collar unions of the past. Their emphasis will be to establish terms and conditions of employment, and at contract time they will act very much like a traditional union—yet with the clout of skilled workers. They will also add new complexity to the workplace, as unions representing bright and curious engineers, scientists, programmers and others second-guess company decisions on such issues as how their pensions are invested.

Tomorrow's union workers may not depend on the union to turn each element of the employment relationship into an actionable grievance. Their highly sought skills will enable them to leave a problematic employer easily. As a result, they will resolve many employment-related issues themselves, just as technical and professional employees do today. Collectively, though, the new unions will advance the interests of their membership, but their goals will be increasingly less oriented to cents per hour and more directed toward fair treatment, work and family, education, training, and other issues of concern to a better-educated and more sophisticated workforce.

Human resource professionals, therefore, will need to learn new skills to handle negotiations and arbitration with these new unions and their new members. Human resource professionals seeking to keep their workplace union-free will have to plan accordingly to anticipate and accommodate workers' wants and needs.

The face of the workplace will change in the twenty-first century. It will be older, more diverse, and more female. There will be fewer qualified workers as the net additions to the workforce decrease. Human resource professionals may find themselves allocating more dollars to their training budgets than ever before to retrain employees when new employees are not available, or to make up for the widening gap between what skills employers will need and what skills are taught in our schools.

As the face of the workplace changes, human resource professionals will continue to grapple with work/life issues. It will become more vital than ever to design a workplace (and with it benefit and compensation packages) that will not only attract and retain scarce workers, but also permit them to contribute in ways that add to their fulfillment of their own potential.

Labor, Social Security, and immigration laws will also have to be changed to reflect the new workforce needs if the United States is to remain an economic world leader. To accomplish these changes, human resource professionals must become a more active voice in reflecting the reality of the workplace of today and tomorrow. More important, they will have to become change-makers, actively participating in the legislative process at both the state and federal levels; few professions are affected as much by legislative changes as is human resource management.

Technology will be another factor to be reckoned with in the twenty-first century. Not only will it demand more skilled workers, it will enable the workplace to become more virtual.

The number of U.S. workers who telecommute has increased in recent years and the trend will continue. Technology will also allow for more workers to become contingent workers, or "free agents." Human resource professionals will have to develop practices that ensure that these workers are "connected" to the workplace by more than just a dedicated line.

Many human resource professionals may find themselves fostering a life-long learning environment in their workplaces to keep workers up-to-date on the myriad technological innovations. This may mean more extensive and cost-effective training programs, or partnerships with local colleges and universities, or both.

Technology will also affect the human resource profession itself. More effective use of the Internet and intranets, and the increasing sophistication of human relations information systems that can effectively track compensation and benefit packages and federal rules and regulations, will demand higher-skilled human resource professionals, while also easing the administrative burdens historically associated with the field. Technology will also permit the increased outsourcing of many of the administrative human resource functions, allowing corporate human resource professionals to become strategic thinkers, planners, and implementers of new ideas and programs.

The workplace of the new millennium will also transcend international borders. The 1990s have witnessed a surge of global mergers and acquisitions, and this globalization will require tomorrow's human resource professionals to consider a whole new set of challenges associated with working in diverse cultures. Language, societal norms, compensation, employment, retirement, and work/family accommodations and expectations are just a few of the issues human resource professionals will have to consider in a global light.

The following chapters in this SHRM-sponsored book provide more detail on the changes—and the challenges—the profession and SHRM face in the new millennium. It is precisely those challenges that will make the human resource profession a vital component in an organization's bottom line.

COMPENSATION AND BENEFITS

Raylana S. Anderson
Compensation and Benefits Committee

Today's most critical Human Resources Compensation and Benefits challenge is the development and ongoing, effective implementation of compensation and benefit programs. These programs must support the desires of both the organization and the employee for individual responsibility and organizational/career connections.

Underlying Issues

Several issues underlie the development of this critical challenge. In 1999 corporations recognized a looming talent shortage at the highest levels. A survey conducted by Byham (1999) reported that the average company expected a 33 percent turnover of its executives in the following five years. One-third of these companies were not confident that they could find suitable replacements. Furthermore, three-fourths of the corporate officers surveyed said that their companies then had insufficient talent or were chronically short of talent.

A final survey finding served to identify the likely long-term impact of this situation. That is, half of the 500 respondents surveyed felt that their companies were not doing effective succession planning and were unprepared to replace key executives (Byham 1999). Certainly, these findings provided information to support a shift in methods of retaining corporate employees, including benefits and compensation practices.

This critical shortage of key management/leadership talent did not occur in a vacuum. For the most part, it resulted from intentional organizational efforts focused on short-term, operational (rather than long-term, strategic) concerns—to control short-term costs, increase short-term productivity, and so forth.

Significant domestic and foreign economic factors (e.g., corporate buy-outs, expansion and uncertainty of international trade and industries, international monetary security, varying labor costs across borders) contributed to organizations' leading their employees and operations down a short-term path.

Organizations in the late 1990s were still stripping out managerial layers and reducing their workforces. The results of these actions included several important practices that have since contributed to the need for change to a long-term, employee-employer relationship based upon meeting both corporate and individual needs.

In the late 1990s, people were working frantically to keep businesses afloat, leaving little or no time and energy to apply a broad perspective on the changing marketplace, customers, and other factors affecting the organization. In this short-term survival mode, businesses were not developing backups for key managerial/leadership roles; they were eliminating "middle" managers and "assistant to" positions (Grossman 1999).

As organizations eliminated middle management roles, individuals remaining at low-level management ranks lost gradual opportunities for growth. And organizations began to recognize seemingly overwhelming gaps between skills needed to progress from one remaining job within the organization to the next (Grossman 1999). As a result, they routinely began to feel it necessary to turn to outside talent to fill top management roles.

As a part of this short-term business focus, supported by the elimination of middle management, organizations increasingly failed to recognize the value of skills (e.g., critical thinking, decision-making, problem-solving) and behaviors (teamwork, collaboration, coaching, developing) that are critical for organizational success in the twenty-first century. Furthermore, individuals who demonstrated these seemingly unusual and short-term unproductive skills were not appropriately rewarded. Corporate rewards, including pay, were provided to individuals with technical skills and competence, often at the expense of, or to the exclusion of, competence in civility and in management/leadership (Grossman 1999).

While these active organizational influences were having an impact on corporate decision-making, other forces also have been at work in the labor market. Women have returned to the workforce in dramatic numbers, and fully 50 percent of today's workforce are women, representing more than 85 percent of all working-age women (Huitt 1998). Employee trends recognized in the late 1990s also are affecting today's organizations. The growth of the labor force has slowed down. The mix of the labor force in terms of race, culture, age, and gender, has changed. People are having children relatively late in life (after they have begun their working careers), forcing work/life choices that are significant to both themselves and their employers. Alternative (i.e., not full-time, regular) employment has continued to develop from the "contingent" workplace ideas of the late 1990s (Rappaport, Bogosian, and Klann 1998).

Several additional trends complete this description of today's work environment and help us recognize important differences between today and the late twentieth century. The pace of change from the agricultural/manufacturing age into the "full" information age continues to accelerate. As of the year 2000, fewer than 13 percent of U.S. workers were involved in agriculture or manufacturing, while more than 50 percent were involved in information (Huitt 1998).

According to Huitt (1998), at the turn of the century, businesses owned by women represented 50 percent of all U.S. businesses. These women-owned businesses were successful and employed more than 18.5 million people—more than 26 percent of the workforce and more people than are employed by all Fortune 500 companies combined. Contrary to then-popular beliefs, the late 1990s demonstrated that women in top management/leadership roles performed well. For example, women's effectiveness as managers, leaders, and teammates outstripped the abilities of their male counterparts in 28 of 31 managerial skill areas (Huitt 1998). Furthermore, workers continuing to enter the workplace today are different from their predecessors. GenXers (now ages 30 to 40) place a high value on education, want technology to support their work, and want time off and work/life flexibility (Rappaport, Bogosian, and Klann 1998). GenYers (now ages 16 to 30) are primary consumers of leisure and entertainment products (Halverson 1998), are more likely than previous generations to express opinions and ask questions, are more accepting of ethnic and cultural differences, are less likely to show prejudice toward races, and are more inclined to demonstrate a sense of personal responsibility (HoraceMann 1996).

In some way, as a reaction to massive corporate job restructuring, layoffs, and reductions in force in the late 1990s, working individuals have exercised their collective strength to influence key legislation and corporate practices. Today's organizational, compensation, and benefits environment is characterized by a Social Security system that includes a significant degree of individual direction on investment of funds, individually portable long-term savings/pension plan benefits, and widespread access to medical savings accounts (MSAs), long-term care (LTC) insurance, and other programs important to individuals.

What Does This Mean Today?

Meeting today's critical compensation and benefits challenges means hard work must continue. It is necessary to develop and implement compensation and benefit programs that support the desires of organizations and employees for both individual responsibility and organizational/career connections. The good news is that a review of these issues and trends can serve as a broad guideline for effective compensation and benefits decision-making in 2010. Furthermore, to meet the challenge, we can build upon the foresight of certain forward-thinking organizations that were beginning to develop compensation, benefits, and work/life practices in the midst of the turmoil outlined above. Broadly, two significant practices are incorporated into today's successful organizational HR roles. One is compensation programs based upon results, and the other is maximum flexibility (i.e., individual responsibility/choice) in benefit program offerings. HR systems, which reinforce individuals' connections to organizations, support these practices on a daily basis. These systems include HR roles to routinely strengthen supervisors' management/leadership skills and to maintain routine contact with individuals who work off-site, off-hours, and so on.

Since the late 1990s, in part through lobbying efforts of SHRM and its members, Congress's attention has moved to recognize and remove regulatory barriers to ongoing organizational and individual success. Congress has acted to eliminate many of these barriers, resulting in a current regulatory environment that provides the following elements:

- Compensation laws and regulations, under a revision of the 1938 Fair Labor Standards Act (FLSA), that support organizational and individual flexibility and responsibility.

- 100 percent deductibility of health-related insurance costs for self-employed individuals.

- Permanent access to medical savings accounts (MSAs).

- Maintenance of tax-favored status for group benefit programs sponsored by organizations.
- Regulations that support cooperation with appropriate levels of liability among businesses, individuals, and communities in support of individual health/wellness.
- Significant levels of both portability of long-term financial/pension benefits, and a level of individual direction of Social Security benefit funds in the financial market.

These regulatory changes support the ability of today's organizations and working individuals to be mutually successful. (The details of their development are not a part of this writing.)

Telework—An Important, Intervening Phenomenon

While Telework is generally viewed as an employment practice, its evolution in modern workplaces has affected decision-making on compensation and benefits. For this reason, a brief description of Telework is important. In describing the "dejobbing" of the workforce, Huitt (1998) established the current description of Telework to include temporary full-time and part-time jobs, home-based business, entrepreneurship, and increased personal responsibility for work. It is important to note that individuals who independently and periodically contract their services to organizations and whose compensation and other rewards are based upon completion of agreed-upon results are included in the Telework/dejobbed workforce.

Compensation Practices

The late 1990s focus on technical skills competence led many organizations to offer compensation packages to individuals that were significantly out of line with established compensation structures. Creativity focused on providing these technology-savvy individuals with more compensation than they could obtain through other sources (i.e., more than they were making at a competitor; more than they might make after a competitive counteroffer; more than they might make if they checked the Web a few weeks from hire).

At the same time that organizations focused on compensation packages for technical skills competence, they began labeling workers as "contingent" nonemployees to avoid organizational compensation and benefit commitments. The Microsoft decision (*Vizcaino v. U.S. District Court for the Western District of Washington*, 1998) and its implications resounded through corporate structure and encouraged individuals to question their work/organizational relationships. In its 1998 *Alternative Staffing Survey*, SHRM reported:

- Nearly three out of four organizations surveyed (74%) used alternative workers to supplement their workforces.
- Nearly eight out of ten respondents (79%) reported that workers from temporary agencies were among their organizations' alternative workers.

Notably, these workers would not, in 1998, have been considered "employees," to whom an organization's own compensation and benefit programs would be offered. In fact, seven out of ten respondents in the SHRM 1998 *Alternative Staffing Survey* said they did not offer any organizational benefits to alternative workers, although these organizations did indicate a preference for using alternative workers from agencies that provided benefits to these individuals. Today, the arbitrary label lines have blurred, and organizations are meeting the compensation and benefits challenges that have been highlighted. As indicated, the broad compensation strategy is to reward individuals based on their performance toward achieving organizational results.

One compensation technique, developed to support compensation for results in a variety of settings and schedules, is the idea of work modules (Coleman 1998). As a practical matter, corporate and HR experience have demonstrated that a four-hour work module is the most effective. Four hours is about the shortest unit of time that is economically or psychologically viable for accomplishing meaningful work.

At appropriate times within corporate staffing evaluation cycles, work is reviewed to determine whether it can be modularized. If modules are appropriate, work, expected results, and related rewards are defined. Individuals within the organization's available, nonregular labor force are notified, and they use a variety of electronic means to offer their services and make commitments to complete available work modules. Compensation professionals monitor this "bidding" process, negotiate final work agreements, monitor timely and accurate completion of the work in cooperation with departmental leaders, and compensate individuals according to agreed-upon parameters. The role of HR professionals within the organization is to support critical connections, as well as to provide important business information.

Module-based work has also been developed as a means of offering work/life flexibility to organizations' regular, full-time employees. Rather than being penalized for missing time "at work," individuals maintain a means for demonstrating work completion/results, regardless of their location. Employees can choose to "leave work" to attend important personal events or meetings and can avoid the negative impact of once-prevalent perceptions that individuals not "at work" were not productive. Results, not face time or location, are the basis for determining productivity and compensation.

Modules are not today's only technique for tying compensation to performance/ results. Compensation and employment professionals in today's organizations cooperate to monitor a variety and a multitude of contract relationships with individuals whose formal employment relationship is not with single organizations. These individuals are often established, successful entrepreneurs whose skills, whether in technical or management/leadership arenas, are valuable to complete a specific project or for a specified period. Bringing these individuals into an organization is a matter of negotiating time, fees, authority, responsibility, and expected results. HR/compensation professionals monitor these negotiations, which are successful only if they are based upon clear communication of expectations and responsibilities.

Compensation decision-making has also been affected by organizations' ongoing development of continuous learning environments, including "corporate universities," an increasingly popular and meaningful benefit plan. These universities have been created in an effort to retain GenXers who expect opportunities for continuous education, to develop technical as well as management/leadership skills in employees and staff pool participants, to support leadership succession management, and, at times, to generate revenue outside of the organization.

The completion of training or development programs within the university or other organizational learning structure is the responsibility of individuals. They review organizational goals and plans and then select a training/development curriculum. It is the responsibility of compensation professionals, in cooperation with employment/training staff and top executives, to monitor training programs and related employee/individual rewards. It is each individual's responsibility to review the available curriculum, enroll, and complete specific programs. Compensation is one reward that has been built into individuals' completion of courses.

Benefits

No longer is the privatizing of some portion of an individual's Social Security benefits major news; the practice is now routine. Employers have been assured, through legislation and accompanying regulations and court decisions, that education for their employees about available Social Security investment options can be provided without liability. For individuals in today's workforce, efforts to make long-term financial plans, including pensions, truly portable, have also been successful.

These practices, along with equity in the full deductibility of health and related insurance costs for self-employed individuals, supports organizations' ability to meet today's challenges. The work/life needs of increasingly diverse employees pushed the trend toward individual choice and responsibility, and flexibility in benefits and non-financial rewards, to tidal wave proportions.

As of 1998, the *SHRM Benefits Survey* reported that flexible benefits (i.e., full cafeteria plans) were offered by just 29 percent of U.S. organizations. The growing and sustained value of flexible benefit programs provided the opportunity to create a win-win situation between organizations and individuals. As a result:

- Organizations maintain the ability to budget total benefit expense by offering eligible individuals a certain sum of dollars from which benefit selections may be made from among those provided by the organization.

- Eligible individuals have the responsibility for learning about available selections and for making appropriate choices.

The same 1998 *SHRM Benefits Survey* documented only initial creativity in offerings of family-friendly, personal service benefits. These benefit offerings were relatively new in 1998 and were initiated to support employees' desires for opportunities to meet work/life objectives (e.g., more "free" time). Meeting these needs also has provided opportunities for organizations to connect with individuals.

Benefit offerings noted in the 1998 *SHRM Benefits Survey* included the following:

Benefit Plan	Percent of Employers Offering the Plan
Dependent care spending accounts	59%
Health care premium spending accounts	46%
Medical flexible spending accounts	57%
Domestic partner benefits	7%
Adoption assistance	12%
Relocation benefits (spousal assistance)	67% (23%)
Long-term care insurance	32%
Educational assistance	87%
Retirement planning services	40%

Note: Adapted with permission from Society for Human Resource Management, *SHRM Benefits Survey*, 1998, pp. 11–42.

In addition to increasing the prevalence of benefit plans, today's benefit programs have been developed to incorporate features and tools that support meeting this critical challenge. Benefit professionals have designed and implemented programs that maximize the application of regulatory flexibility and tax-preferred arrangements. Programs now include comprehensive, ongoing communication to employees about the availability and value of benefits offered to them.

Special plans are incorporated into benefit programs to support mutually productive employer/employee connections. One example is a comprehensive disease management plan that incorporates individual medical support while an individual is unable to work and HR/benefit return-to-work coaching for individuals who have been off of work because of catastrophic illnesses or injuries.

Continuing a trend begun in the 1990s, eldercare and childcare, as well as health/wellness programs, are offered in cooperation with viable community organizations and resources. Coverage in group health benefit plans, with support from the insurance industry, state legislatures, and Congress, routinely includes coverage for "alternative" treatments such as therapeutic massage, acupuncture, herbs, nutritional counseling, guided meditation, and over-the-counter drugs. Childcare and/or eldercare, and an increasing array of personal/concierge services, are routinely offered by today's employers.

As described above, training/development has been incorporated into a true organizational benefit program that supports individual learning. Curricula are routinely monitored to be sure available programs include those that are:

- important to organizations (e.g., basic organizational business and financial programs).

- important to both organizations and individuals (e.g., management, team-building, leadership programs).

- important to individuals with necessary ambition, interests, and abilities. These programs may include technical courses on subjects directly related to individuals' jobs or may provide opportunities for individuals to continue learning about any number of topics.

Nonfinancial reward programs are still being created. These personal benefits have grown in type and number from those offered in the late 1990s (e.g., childcare/eldercare referral service; wellness resources and information; casual dress days; concierge services; dry cleaning services). Individual choices are routinely encouraged, through use of paid time off (PTO) banks. Key employees with outside interests (e.g., community, education) are retained, in part, through opportunities for time off of work for community and related service and through both paid and unpaid sabbaticals. The availability of other benefit plans has grown in support of employee retention efforts and meeting today's critical challenge.

Aspects of employee assistance programs (EAPs), which have been available for years, have been incorporated into the fabric of organizations. Externally, EAPs continue to offer personal counseling services to employees and other staff to meet a variety of needs. Internally, EAP-like benefit plans have been created. Professionals offering services within these plans offer organizations, employees, and staff services to meet the specific challenge of promoting connections.

The primary value offered by an EAP benefit program is maintaining and strengthening necessary connections within organizations. These benefit professionals create and monitor individual executive coaching in succession management. They may also interact with employees to watch for, and work through, signs of burnout before an individual leaves the organization. Responsibilities of organizational EAP professionals may also include delivery of daily services to all individuals whose work is related to the organization.

Orientation is a benefit program that lasts six months to one year. During this period, individuals are provided specialized, one-on-one attention to attach them to the organization. At the same time, organizations clearly outline expectations for the individual. Such expectations focus on each individual's responsibilities, which may include:

- meeting performance expectations.

- active participation in work, whether work is done with or without the cooperation of team members.

- dedication to set and meet progressive educational training and development objectives, through participation in external and/or internal programs.

Summary

The workforce is more diverse than ever, and this diversity continues to shape external and regulatory change, as well as private, organizational change. Those organizations that recruit, retain, and develop managers/leaders to look ahead, plan for meeting the pace of change, and lead and develop the individuals around them will succeed. A significant part of that success will be the implementation of compensation programs based on results and benefit programs that support individual responsibility, choice, and flexibility.

The specific challenge for HR professionals in this field is to maintain and blend sound business knowledge with human behavior and technical skills/competence.

Recommended Actions

Universals

- Know your key business objectives.
- Know your employees' key needs, wants, and motivators.

Compensation/Benefits

- Create and maintain a comprehensive, flexible, total compensation program.
- Blend critical recruiting and training (technical and management) into a total compensation perspective.
- Focus rewards (compensation, benefits) on work (i.e., productivity, results), not on face time. Communicate with all employees and train them to accept and understand this focus.
- Ensure constant communication with all employees and affiliated individuals (when they are working with your company).
- Monitor research on effectiveness of "alternative" and preventive health care. Adopt periodic changes to your plans.
- Remember and plan means to benefit employees with families, as well as singles. Consider plans (e.g., use of paid time off) that support personal commitment to professional or community organizations.
- Develop and monitor databases of available, competent independent contractors. Maintain contact with them (as a part of their reward structure). Develop electronic (i.e., efficient) means to announce available work, accept "bids," and monitor/compensate for results.
- Monitor work to identify modules. Compensate and reward completion of modules appropriately.
- Incorporate comprehensive (chronic) disease—and health—management into group benefit plans.
- Monitor the impact of total compensation programs, including employee satisfaction, as well as costs and utilization. Build individual flexibility/responsibility into the program.

References

Byham, W. C. "Grooming next-millennium leaders." *HR Magazine* 44(2) (1999): 46-70.

Coleman, D. R. "Baby boom to baby bust: Flexible work options for older workers." *Benefits Quarterly*, 14(4) (1998): 18-28.

Grossman, R. J. "Heirs unapparent." *HR Magazine*, 44(2) (1999): 36-44.

Halverson, G. "Power buyers: Boomers and generation Y." *Christian Science Monitor*, 9 March 1998 [on-line]. Available at www.csmonitor.com/durable/1998/03/09/econ/econ.6.html).

HoraceMann Educators Corporation. 1996 educator survey fact sheet [on-line]. Available at www.horacemann.com/html/educator/esurvey7.html).

Huitt, W. G. "The workplace and the transition to the information age: How it impacts and is impacted by women." Paper presented at the 3rd Annual Women's Studies Conference, Valdosta, Georgia, March 1998.

Rappaport, A. M.; Bogosian, C. A; and Klann, C. A. "Population trends and the labor force in the years ahead." *Benefits Quarterly* 14(4) (1998): 8-17.

Society for Human Resource Management Issues Management Program. *SHRM Benefits Survey.* Alexandria, Virginia: Society for Human Resource Management, 1998.

Society for Human Resource Management Issues Management Program. *SHRM Alternative Staffing Survey.* Alexandria, Virginia: Society for Human Resource Management, 1998.

Vizcaino v. U.S. District Court for the Western District of Washington, No. 98-71388 (W.D. Wash. 1998).

Supplemental Readings

Pritchard, K. H. *Telework: Compensation Issues.* SHRM White Paper #61512. Alexandria, Virginia: Society for Human Resource Management, December 1998.

Pritchard, K. H. *Telework: Selected references and resources.* SHRM White Paper #61515. Alexandria, Virginia: Society for Human Resource Management, December 1998.

REINVENTING PUBLIC POLICY THROUGH STATE AND LOCAL CONTROL

Debbra M. Buerkle
Legislative Action Committee

In the 1990s, changes in federal laws dominated the reading material of in-baskets for HR directors nationwide. The pendulum is swinging back, and HR professionals will see an increased volume of local ordinances and state laws governing how they define and carry out employment policy and employee-employer relationships. Since 1994, passage of employment-related laws at the state level has increased dramatically. HR professionals should prepare to face a continued surge of "customized" public policy geared to legislate how employers "do business" at the state and local levels.

What is causing this shift from nearly exclusive federal policymaking to high-gear production and dissemination of state and local public policy affecting employment? According to Edward Potter's (1995, p. 6) white paper, "No longer can competitiveness be viewed as a macroeconomic contest between nations. It is a struggle fought daily by employers and employees in the operating units of American companies."

In the 1930s and 1940s, when competitiveness affected our national economic viability and military security, many of the original employment-related regulations affecting employers, including Social Security and the Fair Labor Standards Act, were put into place. Also, the federal government was vigorously working to effect economic and social reform. Why use employers as the vehicle for these reforms? It is allowed under the Interstate Commerce clause of the Constitution. Employers have money and also have influence at the local level. Our government knows it can't afford to continue its efforts to enact and enforce social change by being the "national enforcer"—it must shift the burden by encouraging state and local governments and agencies to carry out the social, economic, and political agendas of the times.

The Occupational Safety and Health Administration (OSHA) is an example of an agency that has made a shift from enforcement to encouragement. Most recently, the agency introduced administrative changes ushering in a customer-friendly approach to enforcement and compliance that provides incentives to local agencies for effecting goals at the local level. In fact, a press release (1998) from OSHA announcing its new award-winning enforcement partnership program also reported that the agency was expanding nationwide as the cooperative compliance program (CCP) and that it was being offered to 12,250 employers. OSHA's Maine 200 program, the prototype for CCP, won the prestigious Innovation in American Government Award from the Ford Foundation as well as the Hammer Award from Vice President Al Gore's National Performance Review in 1998. While some say this is just another method of enforcing a federally mandated agenda, others pronounce the trend "effective" because it is happening within and through local control. Regardless of whether it's effective, it is demonstrating the shift from federal control to regionalized control.

Another reason for the shift is pressure arising from American small businesses to specifically address their social and economic concerns. It is likely that laws and ordinances will be developed to fuel the continued growth and competitive opportunity afforded these smaller businesses. According to the National Federation of Independent Businesses (NFIB) (1999):

> Congress and the president need to be more aware of the fact that the burden of federal regulations falls disproportionately on small business. The idea of one-size-fits-all regulation is unrealistic and costly. In fact, the regulatory cost per employee to small firms is approximately 50 percent more than the cost to large firms. Small businesses employ 53 percent of the work force, but shoulder 63 percent of the total business regulatory costs. Firms with 20 to 49 employees spend, on average, 19 cents out of every revenue dollar on regulatory costs. When we hear "regulations" we don't necessarily remember all of the paperwork that comes with them. Tax compliance and payroll record keeping are the two largest components of the regulatory burden today. Firms with less than 10 employees report that their tax and payroll costs represent about 80 percent of their total regulatory burden. In fact, firms with under 50 employees spend close to five percent of their revenue on tax compliance costs alone.

Local governments also have pressures to compete. In recent years, cities and counties have created their own minimum wage requirements (enforced with businesses that provide services and resources to those local government entities) to ensure competitiveness with larger employers or unions.

In order to be responsive to their constituents, state legislatures are contending with questions of employment practices such as reference-checking, employee conduct (violence in the workplace), credit-checking, retraining welfare and displaced workers, and English-only language use in the workplace. Another trend at the state level, a proliferation of benefit mandates for insurers and employers, makes doing business across state lines an administrative nightmare. Discussion is also prevalent about local ordinances supporting or disallowing discrimination based on sexual orientation. All of these topics, and more, will be evaluated for applicability in the workplace at the local or regional level because of pressures from both local governments and businesses residing in and operating within that state.

How will human resources be affected by the increased state and local attempts to define and customize public employment policy in a way that more directly serves local constituencies? The following are six ways:

1. **Employers will put increased pressure on their HR leadership to participate in grassroots efforts to design legislation favorable to their industry or core business at the state and local levels.** HR profession advocates will find themselves needing to form coalitions and alliances with existing state and local public policy influences, such as the Chamber of Commerce, in order to formulate effective policy initiatives or responses to proposed legislation. Individuals who think that grassroots participation is a waste of time will be left in the dust of those who race forward to create controls that are favorable for their *businesses*.

2. **More emphasis will be placed on *where profits originate* (to prevent an erod-ed tax base in the wake of Internet/global commerce), forcing different ways of compensating and accounting for workforce production and productivity.** Legislation governing payroll and sales taxes at the state and local levels will increase to prevent the erosion of the regional tax base. Look for local respons-es to Internet commerce, especially the question of what's taxable, and which governments benefit from that taxation.

3. **Nearly every HR professional will need "international" experience and pro-fessional resources supporting doing business with non-U.S. business partners, contractors, and employees.** Right now, we're seeing an increase in cities creating a "living" or minimum wage for payment of employees living locally or doing business with a local government. As global competitiveness increases and a "local" company's workforces and product distribution net-works extend globally, HR professionals may be tracking much more than just U.S.-legislated regional "living wage" requirements; they'll have to have access to and be able to respond to wage and benefit issues in every region of the world.

4. **The changes in workforce demographics will render many U.S. discrimination laws useless, especially if employees are citizens of, and residing in, other countries while working for your firm.** These changes will encourage a prolif-eration of new laws governing how local/state-based firms must treat local and nonlocal workers. They will include which employees are considered part of the local workforce, and therefore are subject to local employment practice legislation (especially the aging workforce). This will also mean significant leg-islative reactions to the intergeneration equity issues that will emerge as the "boomer" generation continues to age. According to the U.S. Census Bureau, America's older population will more than double by 2050, from 33.9 million to 80 million. By that year, as many as one in five Americans could be senior citizens, and many of those will still be active in the workforce.

5. **Futurists and HR professionals seem to agree that businesses will continue to stay slim by assigning functions to subcontractors. Because more people will be paid from individual or small-business employment contracts, questions about which/whose laws apply to those contracts must be answered.** Legislation at the state and local levels will most likely be what raises these questions. And most likely, the HR professional will be the one to answer them. Think of this situation: A software development firm is having difficulty finding the requisite-skilled employees it needs. It finds a variety of skilled "free agents" and contracts for their time and work product individually from where they live in Malaysia, Singapore, Pakistan, and Romania. Work products and communication about work are sent back and forth over the Internet, or by phone or fax. Your company is going to be more concerned about ques-tions of security, contractual compliance, work-product ownership, and product quality than with questions about timekeeping and exempt/nonex-empt status. "Traditional" Department of Labor wage and hour concerns may not even be relevant anymore. This is a very real situation, and if it's not

already happening in your organization, it probably will be soon. HR professionals will need to develop creative *and* compliant strategies to address global business issues affecting their profession and their organization.

6. **HR professionals will need to align more closely with local medical professionals and insurance professionals servicing their workforce in order to comply with a proliferation of more vigorous laws supporting healthy ecosystems within and around the workplace—and not just "the" workplace, but all workplaces used by your workers.** This will especially be necessary in states that legislate 24-hour benefit programs (those plans that cover both personal and occupational-related medical conditions) to adequately insure the huge population of home-based businesses. Insurance portability issues and health care plan eligibility (especially with regard to community and age-based underwriting) will be increasingly legislated at the local and regional levels in order to respond to the needs of smaller, entrepreneurial businesses.

Exploring these six areas in more depth highlights the readiness and responsiveness of HR professionals.

1. **HR professionals will face increased pressure to participate in grassroots efforts to design legislation favorable to their industry or core business at the state and local levels.**

   Competencies required:

   (a) Cognizance of your organization's industry trends and resources, and a comprehensive local personal contact network to tap into the local and regional legislative process. For example, a manufacturer of computer peripheral equipment will have industry ties to the American Electronics Association (AEA), the local employers' association, and the local Chamber of Commerce. HR professionals in this type of industry sector would need to be grassroots participants within the local Chamber and should be familiar with the lobby supporting the AEA at the state level.

   (b) Good networking skills, as well as the ability to find and filter information pertaining to the HR profession within your particular industry.

   (c) A clear understanding of the legislative infrastructure in your state, county, and city governments.

   (d) The ability to develop and maintain positive relationships with industry sector representatives and professional lobbyists in order to keep abreast of legislation affecting your employer.

2. **HR professionals will be required to understand *where profits originate* (to prevent an eroded tax base in the wake of Internet/global commerce) and to develop different ways of compensating and accounting for workforce production and productivity.**

   Competencies required:

   (a) A comprehensive understanding of the business strategy affecting your organization.

(b) An ability to find, discern, and use compensation data resources in a way that integrates effectively with productivity and quality concerns of the organization.

(c) An understanding of the laws, both local/regional and federal, affecting compensation design and delivery.

(d) An understanding of tax law as it relates to profitability in the organization, as well as to compensation *and benefits*.

3. **Nearly every HR professional will need "international" experience and professional resources supporting doing business with non-U.S. business partners, contractors, and employees.**

Competencies required:

(a) An ability to discern and secure applicable data and resources pertaining to other countries' national and regional compensation and practices, as well as a knowledge of any non-U.S. laws that govern doing business within other countries where the your organization or employees may be located.

(b) A comprehensive resource person available to assist with development of contracts and contractor agreements with nationals from other parts of the world.

(c) An understanding of the applicability of benefits programs to employees or contractors within those countries where your firm does business.

4. **The changes in workforce demographics will render many U.S. discrimination laws useless, especially if employees are citizens of and residing in other countries while working for your firm. The aging of the U.S. workforce will lead to legislation affecting intergeneration equity.**

Competencies required:

(a) An understanding of your region/state and city's demographics and your organization's commitment to reflect those demographics.

(b) An understanding of the impact of an aging workforce on scheduling, ergonomic, and workplace health and safety requirements, and essential functions.

(c) An understanding of multi-audience communication problems and the ability to develop innovative approaches to ensure understanding of company policy and communiqués throughout the organization.

(d) The ability to discern the impact of diverse demographics on your organization's training and development needs, and especially the cultural expectations relating to interpersonal relationship skills.

(e) An ability to discern and communicate the potential impact of proposed changes in EEO regulations and legislation on your organization *before* changes in legislation occur.

5. **Businesses will continue to stay slim by assigning functions to subcontractors. Because more people will be paid from individual or small-business employment contracts, questions about which/whose laws apply to those contracts must be answered.**

Competencies required:

(a) An understanding of current tax codes and laws affecting contractor relationships.

(b) The ability to develop and maintain effective and fair policies and practices affecting contractor relationships within your organization.

(c) The ability to discern your organization's or industry's needs with regard to use of subcontractors, small businesses, and *minority enterprises and the ability to locate and assist in prequalifying these resource providers for contracting purposes.*

6. **HR professionals will need to align more closely with local medical professionals and insurance professionals servicing their workforce in order to comply with a proliferation of more vigorous laws supporting healthy ecosystems within and around the workplace.**

Competencies required:

(a) A thorough understanding of the work environments affecting your organization's employees.

(b) A thorough understanding of the risk factors affecting those environments.

(c) The ability to discern preventative approaches to reducing risk in each of the applicable work environments.

(d) An understanding of the laws and regulations applying to your organization's work environments.

It's always difficult to hold up the crystal ball and prognosticate events—especially where politics are involved. But the trend of increased state and local legislation and regulatory impact will continue. This will happen in part as a response to perceived federal overregulation, but more likely as the federal government itself scales back efforts to promulgate national-level controls and looks to the states to provide the funds and the labor to carry out policies that will effect social and political change. On behalf of their profession, and the businesses they represent, HR professionals will be increasingly challenged to respond to legislation and controls proposed at the state and local levels.

Recommended Actions

- Identify and monitor resources that publish demographic statistics for your metropolitan statistical area or region.
- Know your state legislators and their staff.

- Bookmark federal and state legislative information sites and monitor their summaries on the Internet.
- Maintain your membership in SHRM and become a grassroots member.
- Join the local Chamber of Commerce and maintain relationships with that group's members.
- Know your congressional representatives and their staff.
- Never assume that you can't make an impact on public policy.
- Attend your city council or county commissioners meetings periodically.
- Keep a file of newspaper, trade journal, and other research source news that highlights employment-related public policy issues at the state, local, and federal levels.
- Network with people to discuss trends and ascertain public opinion that may influence grassroots legislation, and stay involved!

References

National Federation of Independent Businesses. "What ever happened to regulatory reform?" February 1999 [on-line]. Available at http://www.nfibonline.com.

Occupational Safety and Health Administration press release. 1998. [on-line]. Available at http://www.osha.gov/media/oshnews.

Potter, E. *The Proper Federal Role in Workplace Policy.* White paper. Washington, D.C.: Center for Employment Policy, 1995.

COMPETENCY-BASED APPROACH TO LEVERAGING TALENT*

Robyn Burke
Human Resource Development Committee

Introduction: Skills Shortage Magnified

As competitive pressures, the pace of change, technological innovation, and the fast flow of information continue to increase, so does the demand for specialized knowledge and skills. Consequently, human resource professionals must address an intensifying challenge to attract and retain capable, qualified human resources. With this dynamic business environment, employers are forced to take creative, aggressive measures to persevere through the labor shortage difficulties and to build the competencies required for the future. The greatest challenges are the absence of skilled workers and an aging and increasingly mobile workforce.

Clearly, there are not enough skilled workers to fill the 1,239,557 job vacancies (America's Job Bank 1999). The majority of these job opportunities will continue to be within the professional/specialty/technical occupations. Futurists predict that 60 percent of all jobs will require skills possessed by only 20 percent of today's workforce (Saratoga Institute 1997, as cited by Interim Services 1999). Computer-related and teaching jobs will comprise more than 15 percent of all new jobs between 1996 and 2006. And of the twenty-five fastest growing occupations, eighteen will require a minimum of a bachelor's degree (Pilot 1998). The gap between current skills and needed skills is widening. This skill shortage is resulting in a constant requirement and market for talent (Talent Alliance, as cited by Interim Services 1999).

In addition, because our labor pool is older, the widening of the gap is accelerating. The number of workers ages forty and older is growing at a rapid rate, with a significant number in the over-fifty-five population. The increasing percentage of available workers over age fifty-five has caused the labor pool to grow at a snail's pace. Most businesses today do not tap into the talent available through this older, but very employable, resource. The resulting challenge for employers today is how to create a large enough pool of skilled workers.

Retention: A Compelling Issue

Before you develop a human resource strategy that will best equip you to attract and develop the necessary talent, consider not only the challenge of finding the skills in a labor market that is falling way behind, but also how to keep and leverage this qualified pool when you need it. Retention, career development, and sources for finding the talent in a timely manner have a major impact on your ability to tap into a talent pool when needed.

* The author would like to thank Diana Osinski, Shelly Prochaska, and Jack Kondrasuk, members of SHRM's national Human Resource Development Committee, for their support, ideas, and assistance in writing, researching, and editing this chapter.

Retention presents greater challenges than ever before; 280 million workers have changed jobs since 1980. Labor is being redeployed at an unprecedented scale and pace, straining the current system and threatening corporations' abilities to execute their business strategies. In this market, highly skilled employees see themselves as free agents. They are a scarce, and therefore costly, resource (Saratoga Institute 1997, as cited by Interim Services 1999). Because of their scarcity, recruiting and sourcing talent has become a huge business of its own.

The sources for qualified workers to perform core business processes and key business support services are many and varied, and tapping them is necessary to bridge the wide gap. Workers are being obtained from many nontraditional labor and recruiting sources because of the labor shortage, including use of immigrants, exporting/packaging of work, outsourcing, and use of contingent workers. These sources translate to means of survival for employers coping with the deficiency of knowledge and skills.

The Human Resource Development Strategy of the Twenty-First Century

The above factors are contributing to the greatest human resources challenge for the twenty-first century—specifically, how can essential talent and skills be leveraged in this fluctuating market with a severe shortage of qualified workers who look older and are harder to find and keep? This complex labor market has forced businesses to take creative measures to tackle the challenge. It has shifted the role of human resources from a back room support function to a key contributor in achieving crucial business results. Knowledge has become the only source of long-term, sustainable, competitive advantage, but knowledge can only be employed through the skills of individuals (Horne 1998).

Tapping this knowledge base means everything. Wallace (1998), as cited by Verespej (1998), maintained that organizations continue to combine emerging technologies with creative employment arrangements, contingency-based pay, customer and supplier partnerships, and other mechanisms that enable them to tap seamlessly into talented employees anywhere at anytime. This new, emerging workforce is more complex. There are core workers who possess the requisite knowledge and skills to deliver key business process; hired guns who specialize in certain technologies or support processes; and contingent workers who serve to supplement the core workforce during peaks and valleys. Therefore, today's employee has many options as to how to relate to a company (Verespej 1998). And companies have to plan strategically how to optimize this workforce mix in such a way as to leverage the right talent at the right time.

Focus Your Human Resource Development Strategy on Competency-Building

The net result of these challenges is that employers are faced with making a strategic decision. Employers must consider what spot along the competency development spectrum best suits their needs. Will you:

- contribute to the continuing inequitable workforce situation by narrowing consideration of who is employable? This choice perpetuates the undereducation, lack of skills, and barriers for the older worker.

- proactively develop a compelling strategy to engage and ensure that the potential work pool obtains critical education and knowledge and that these people become a large percentage of the labor pool?

The choices employers make today will determine their success in 2020 and, to a great extent, affect both the U.S. and world economies. Therefore, employers must assume leadership to ensure the existence of a capable workforce.

A proactive strategy begins with organizations assessing and recognizing what they are not and being willing to reassign less strategic, noncore processes. At the same time, they must fully dedicate the development of their internal human resources toward building competencies that will equip them to maintain a competitive advantage in serving customers.

So what is a competency? Be sure that your organizational members and human resources practitioners agree on its definition and application. It is more than knowledge, skills, talent, and attributes; it is a cluster or an accumulation of any and all of the above. The distinguishing element is that a competency correlates directly to the successful (or unsuccessful) performance of a job, role, or responsibility. What distinguishes a competency is that it address whether a person will be able to perform in a certain situation. Thus, it can be measured against well-accepted standards and can be improved through training and development (Parry 1998).

A focused, competency-based approach allows businesses to identify activities and services that are not essential to the business. Once identified, these services become prime candidates for outsourcing, exporting, or use of contingent workers or other sources that do possess and attract those necessary talents and skills. The suppliers of these secondary processes have the freedom to focus on cultivating core competencies that are required to deliver business support services (Sharp 1997).

When you tap into these nontraditional talent sources for the delivery of noncore processes, the outside service providers may offer a career path, appropriate and timely training, and a competitive compensation package to leverage the essential knowledge and skills needed to develop an organization's set of core competencies. Consequently, this partnership approach allows organizations to gain access to individuals with specialized skills that an employer might otherwise find both expensive and difficult to attract. Because there is a shortage of skilled workers, and skilled workers tend to be ambitious, they are more likely to take jobs that offer career paths, training, challenging assignments, and self-development (Sharp 1997). Furthermore, this partnership approach allows these support service providers to invest in building a larger qualified pool.

The Impact of Your Choice

The most important implication of these workforce challenges to businesses today is that they force employers to create mechanisms that permit individuals to be upwardly mobile. The quality of the future labor pool depends on the knowledge and skills acquired by today's students. Employers have a compelling interest in the health of the educational system (SHRM Visions 1998) and its capacity to develop this knowledge base. A nation with a large number of workers who are unemployable or capable of working only in the most menial, low-wage jobs will be a nation fraught with social tension and burdened by expensive demands of social welfare programs. The driving force of upward mobility depends simply on education— education that starts in the public school system (D'Amico 1997) and continues diligently with employers.

Acknowledging that the largest percentage of the labor pool is underskilled gives employers a reason to consider seriously how to engage this untapped source. Businesses that endeavor to tap into this underutilized segment of the workforce will be the premier employers in 2020. The solution is not new or complex. Specifically, employers need to consider the urgency of the following:

- Employees are the learning capacity of organizations.

- Underskilled and older workers are a crucial source of untapped talent.

- Learning opportunities develop the competencies of lower-skilled employees and enable them to become key contributors to the core processes.

- Literacy programs, skills training, and interesting project work engage individuals and enable them to learn.

- Motivating and retaining the *entire* team, both the employees from within the company and the employees from outside sources is critical. Providing incentives and recognition for the "outsiders" is not practiced by many employers, but it is crucial to achieving desired results, and therefore it needs to be included in the retention strategy.

Whether the job is for the core employer or the supplier of business support services, individuals require a broader set of competencies beyond reading, writing, math, solving basic problems, and behaving dependably. Today, more than 50 percent of jobs require more than these basic skills, and the percentage will continue to grow. The broader set, which can be developed through multiple learning experiences, includes managing more complex projects through defining problems; quickly assimilating relevant data; reorganizing information; discussing findings; and working collaboratively with others to find, develop, and implement the best solutions (Mower 1997).

Employers who accept the critical responsibility to provide learning opportunities for developing both the basic and broader sets of competencies will boost overall employability. That is, they will create the capability for attracting, constructing, and developing productive skills and competencies that will allow individuals to find, initiate, and enrich jobs, and thus to obtain rewarding careers (Ducci IFTDO). Now the proposition shifts to how best to boost employability with a labor pool that is not skilled enough, is older, is more mobile, and is retained from multiple external sources.

Target the Talent and Develop It

The answer is to focus human resource development opportunities around key processes. Depending on the type of business, key processes may be manufacturing of specific products, researching and developing of products, packaging of products, or sales and marketing. The time has come to commit to identifying and developing the set of competencies needed through offering an appropriate blend of learning opportunities. It requires an approach that targets the underlying competencies needed to achieve high performance and later provides the necessary skills-building. The competencies will lay the solid foundation needed for effective skills instruction (Parry 1998). In addition, such a commitment demands the engagement of external sources to allow access to competencies required to deliver supporting services.

Use a Competency-Based Approach to Human Resource Development

Given the complexity, diversity, and global nature of the emerging workforce, coupled with the shortage of skilled workers, employers are facing challenges to ensure that the necessary skills are there when needed. Where should an organization begin? The best place to start is to assess and decide which three to five processes are core to the business. Once these are clearly defined and understood, begin structuring the talent of the organization around those processes so that individuals focus on the calibration and improvement of those processes. In addition to organizing the human resources, consider the possibility of introducing information solutions and software to process and rearrange the workflow and talent (Verespej 1998). As a result of focusing on the core processes, companies can target the competencies/talents needed to enable them to achieve business results. Furthermore, companies may utilize other workforce talent sources such as immigration, exportation of work, contingent workers, or outsourcing to contend with the many less important, but necessary, processes.

The goal is to ensure access to an adequately qualified labor pool and to cultivate the talent needed in a tough, tight, competitive market. This can only be accomplished by focusing on what the business is and needs to be all about. Furthermore, it means allowing other businesses to make a living by delivering the less important or specialized processes. The less important processes are likely to be some other organization's core processes, such as sales and marketing, packaging, researching or analyzing, or delivering. It can be costly to "give up" these secondary processes, but not as costly as trying to sustain the capability internally.

This competency-based approach allows employees to be trained and to enjoy careers with either the "core" company or the supplier company, which by virtue of supplying one of the noncore processes has a core of its own. Both employers in this scenario have a tremendous opportunity to attract, hire, retain, develop, motivate, and leverage a talent pool of workers. Both employers have careers to offer to workers. A focus on key processes provides a clear definition of the set of competencies required for success.

Agencies supplying temporary workers, and businesses themselves, have a responsibility to operate schools and training facilities to address skill gaps, notably in the skilled blue-collar labor area. The development activities need to include short courses, training, and certification to meet that demand (Coates 1997). Suppliers that are used to bridge the skills gap in the computer-related field must develop a rigorous plan for growing the talent pool. Therefore, the combined provision of training and project learning experiences will enable these organizations to test, certify, and meet the quality standards required by the organization's client base. These combined learning experiences may open the door to career opportunities for the underemployed, older, and underskilled labor pool.

Equip Contributors with the Competencies to Flex

As mentioned earlier, the broader competency set required by most businesses today is the ability to flex with changes by managing successfully in a complex, multiple-project-based environment. We are witnessing the disappearance of the job as we know it. People are assigned to projects or programs rather than jobs. A job will consist of working on a project or program for a certain period of time, instead of doing the same tasks routinely and repeatedly (Verespej 1998). Many routine tasks have been or will be automated, or are/will be provided by a supplier who can perform those tasks more efficiently. Therefore, using projects as a training ground for project management skill development optimizes the transfer of learning to the workplace and at the same time provides professional skill development and the achievement of business and operational objectives. Employers must be savvy about providing this education and establishing parameters for the type and selection of appropriate projects, project sponsorship, and learning goals. The project management skill set has rapidly become the critical competency set for individuals to achieve high performance of core processes. Employers need to have the flexibility and elasticity to assign individuals to different projects throughout their careers.

Employers and individuals must take joint responsibility for developing the core competencies. Those interested in becoming contributors and enhancing skills will require a rigorous learning plan. The plan may include development through formal training and certification, challenging projects, mentoring, and self-paced learning via tools such as interactive multimedia-based training, video/satellite technology, and Web-based training. These tools can incorporate situational responses and help assess and develop competencies. Before an individual can participate in pursuing these learning opportunities, employers must help by providing training on how to utilize these resources effectively and implementing creative solutions for gaining access to them.

The Employers' Responsibility

This chapter has examined the many challenges employers face today. The reality is that employers have to do more to continue education and improve the employability and upward mobility of the unskilled workforce, whose demographic makeup presents an additional challenge of its own. The recommendations for leveraging the talents and skills required in this highly professional technical workplace stem from taking a fundamental and diligent review of the businesses' core processes and the set of competencies needed to deliver those processes. Thereafter, the emphasis is about retaining and developing the competencies around these processes.

Use Competencies to Integrate Your HRD Strategy to the Business Strategy

The approaches are similar whether you are an employer providing the business product or service or a supplier of the support services. Specifically, the human resource development practitioner must:

- demonstrate that human resources are your business' future learning capacity. The "operations group" still might not buy it. With competencies, you will be able to measure the difference in performance results.

- offer formal training, specifically skills instruction, to the extent necessary to deliver core processes successfully. This may include:
  - schools and training facilities.
  - literacy programs such as reading, writing, math, and computer literacy.
  - short courses, certifications, post-secondary education.
  - English as a second language or other languages appropriate to supporting the core business processes.

- focus learning experiences only on the set of competencies needed for high performance of core processes. Let your vendors provide your employees with the peripheral competencies; in fact, require it of them!

- begin with targeting and developing the competencies; gradually introduce skills-building.

- include project management skills development for all employees. This set of competencies, more than any other, is required for today's professional/technical job, which is no longer a job but a series of project assignments. The following learning experiences are recommended:
  - Strengthen problem-solving and decision-making skills through working on practical work problems as a training medium (Kemske 1998).
  - Use project assignments that are interesting enough to motivate and challenging enough to provide additional learning to the employee.
  - Provide access and training on how to use self-paced development tools.
  - Provide project management skills development for all employees involved in outsourcing, supplier partnerships, immigration, or exporting of work.

- tap into the older labor force by including them in all of the above. They are too large to ignore, and they offer tremendous potential toward bridging the skills shortage.

- develop a strategy and process to reeducate or provide additional skills for underskilled individuals or older workers who possess the potential to be key contributors, and who are much more readily available and accessible than the already highly skilled candidates.

In summary, you can expect the human resources challenges to remain constant. Dollars are tighter; competition, and therefore mobility, is greater; and the demographics of the workforce are more diverse than ever. Clearly, the skill shortage is worse than ever. The need for education, knowledge, skills, abilities, and talents is at its highest. The door to opportunity is as wide open as it has ever been, for employers and for the workforce. The gap is large. Now is the time to build bridges. The best place to start is at the beginning. Consider how to build a foundation to sustain your company in 2020. Develop a strategy that integrates the untapped workforce sources and develops the competencies needed to sustain our future. The human resources strategy that proactively, aggressively develops its learning capacity will be best-equipped to meet the next decade's toughest challenges. Most of all, a proactive, aggressive human resources strategy will enable individuals to gain further education and skills and begin filling the desperate need for professional, technical, and specialized workers.

Recommended Actions

- Define the essential, primary processes of your business, and the people requirements needed to deliver those processes.
- Offer formal training, specifically skills instruction, to the extent necessary to retain the needed talent. This may include:
  - schools and training facilities.
  - literacy programs such as reading, writing, math, and computer literacy.
  - short courses, certifications, post-secondary education.
  - English as a second language or other languages appropriate to supporting the core business processes.
- Focus learning experiences only on the set of competencies needed for high performance of core processes. Select vendors who provide the peripheral competencies. In fact require it, contractually!
- Begin with targeting and developing the competencies; gradually introduce skills-building.
- Include project management skills development for all employees. This set of competencies, more than any other, is required for today's professional/technical job, which is no longer a job but a series of project assignments. The following learning experiences are recommended:
  - Strengthen problem-solving and decision-making skills through working on practical work problems as a training medium (Kemske 1998).
  - Use project assignments that are interesting enough to motivate and challenging enough to provide additional learning to the employee.
  - Provide access and training on how to use self-paced development tools.

- Provide project management skills development for all employees involved in outsourcing, supplier partnerships, immigration, or exporting of work.
- Tap into the older labor force by including them in all of the above. They are too large to ignore, and they offer tremendous potential toward bridging the skills shortage.
- Develop a strategy and process to reeducate or provide additional skills for underskilled individuals or older workers who possess the potential to be key contributors, and who are much more readily available and accessible than the already highly skilled candidates.

References

America's Job Bank. 1999. [on-line]. Available at http://www.ajb.dni.us.

Coates, J.F. "Emerging HR issues for the twenty-first century." *Employment Relations Today*, 23(4) (1997): 1–9.

D'Amico, C. "Back to the future: A current view of workforce 2000 and projections for 2020." *Employment Relations Today*, 24(3) (1997): 1–12.

Ducci, M.A. "Training for employability." *International Federation of Training & Development Organisations* [on-line]. Available at http://www.iftdo.org/article1.html.

Horne III, J.F. "The chicken wire factor: The shift to encouraging employee initiative." *Employment Relations Today*, 25(1) (1998): 1–9.

Interim Services In Conjunction With Louis Harris & Associates. *1999 emerging workforce*. 1999. [on-line]. Available at http://www.interim.com.

Kemske, F. "HR 2008: A forecast based on our exclusive study." *Workforce*, 77 (1998) [on-line]. Available at http://www.workforceonline.com/research/index.html.

Mower, E. "That was then, this is now: Passage to a new economy." *Employment Relations Today*, 24(3) (1997): 13–20.

Parry, S. B. "Just what is a competency? (and why should you care?)." *Training* 35(6) (1998): 58–64.

Pilot, M.J. "A review of 50 years of change." In *Occupational Outlook Handbook*, 1998–1999. Washington, D.C.: Bureau of Labor Statistics, 1998, table 1.

Sharp, A.G. "Does training keep up with the times?" *Law & Order* 45(12) (1997): 43.

SHRM Workplace Visions. "U.S. education system." *SHRM Issues Management Program*, Alexandria, Virginia: Society for Human Resource Management, May–June 1998.

Verespej, M.A. "The old workforce won't work." *Industry Week* 247 (21 September 1998): 53-62.

USE AND MISUSE OF GENETIC INFORMATION IN THE WORKPLACE[1]

David F. Bush
Workplace, Health, and Safety Committee

Recent developments in genetic research have created a double-edged sword. On the one side we have the promise of new levels of understanding, detection, prevention, and treatment of human disease. On the other we find a new threat of discrimination in the workplace. Where a genetic basis for disease can be established, prevention, early detection, and treatment all become possible. However, such genetic information can be used to unfairly penalize those individuals who have diagnostic indicators of potential health problems. A major concern is the possible exclusion of people from jobs or benefits because they possess a particular genetic characteristic, even though that trait may have no impact on their ability to perform the job and may even be unexpressed in the individual. Furthermore, given the uneven distribution of genetic traits among racial and ethnic groups, it is possible that such discrimination can occur unevenly, affecting some racial/ethnic groups more than others. Gregor Mendel's[2] classic 1866 paper on the laws of genetic inheritance in pea plants has been misused in the past (Markel 1992), and it appears that it could happen again. This chapter will review the current state to which genetic research presents both potential benefit and potential threat to American workers.

The Potential Benefits of Genetic Research

Progress in identifying the many genes that constitute the human genome has allowed scientists to develop techniques for the detection, prevention, and amelioration of the effects of genetic disease. Genetics investigators have demonstrated that inherited genetic errors lead directly to several thousand diseases, including breast and ovarian cancer, cystic fibrosis, sickle cell anemia, and Huntington disease (Asch, Patton, Hershey, and Mennuti 1993; American Society of Human Genetics 1994; Harper 1992; Council on Ethical and Judicial Affairs 1991). Less precise relationships resulting from multiple genetic errors have been shown to contribute to other serious illnesses such as heart disease and cancer. Genetic research has led to technology which has produced tests that have become increasingly available and can be used to identify people who have a susceptibility to certain illnesses.

There are numerous examples of tests that have been developed for detecting genetic disease. The diseases for which such indicators have been developed include colorectal cancers resulting from defects in the APC gene, Huntington disease, sickle cell anemia, and cystic fibrosis. With the rapid expansion of the Human Genome Project, it is expected that many more tests for genetic disease will be available in the near future.

[1] The author expresses his appreciation to Amy Nowlin Drummond and David Nocek for their assistance in preparing this manuscript.
[2] Gregor Mendel's classic work on genetics was rediscovered in 1900 and contributed to the eugenics movement popular in the first quarter of the twentieth century.

The Human Genome Project

The Human Genome Project is a federally funded project that is attempting to map the human genome. With a budget of more than $3 billion, this 15-year endeavor seeks to determine the sequential location and protein code for each human gene. It is estimated that more than 4,000 hereditary disorders result from single gene defects, and even more result from the interaction of genetic and environmental factors. After the structural map of the human genome is complete, scientists will continue to struggle to understand the function of all genes and the ways in which they are regulated. This approach is expected to dominate the genetics research agenda for decades, as scientists attempt to create order out of this massive array of complex relationships.

Applications of Genetic Research

The primary application of genetic research has been in the area of genetic testing. Five basic types of genetic testing have been distinguished, with each characterized by a distinct application (Dutton 1995). Each test presents an opportunity for genetic information to enter a family's medical record.

1. **Carrier screening** is used to determine the probability of parents' transmission of genetic disease to their children.

2. **Prenatal diagnostic testing** is used to determine if a fetus has a disease-causing gene.

3. **Predisposition testing** determines genetically based vulnerability to diseases and environmental conditions.

4. When a genetic disease is suspected, **confirmatory diagnostic testing** is conducted to confirm its presence.

5. **Forensic and identity testing** is the application of genetic matching to the establishment of paternity and criminal identification.

Genetic screening in the workplace seems to represent a combination of types 3 and 4, either confirming existing conditions or determining vulnerability. Its rationale is generally based in preventive healthcare, according to clinical laboratory companies developing the technology (Dutton 1995). As a service to employees, such screening would permit the targeting of vulnerable individuals for more frequent monitoring to allow detection of such diseases early, when they are more easily treated. It would also permit the counseling of genetically vulnerable individuals to avoid exposure to industrial chemicals that could create health problems. However, such access to the genetic makeup of employees and job applicants also presents the possibility for reducing future healthcare costs for a corporation through selective discriminatory practices.

A second type of genetic testing that can be used in the workplace is genetic monitoring, the repeated testing of an employee's genetic material to determine if it has changed with the passage of time as a result of exposure to hazardous substances in the workplace. If a population of employees with a specific substance exposure display evidence of above-chance change in genetic materials, appropriate health and safety precautions can be introduced, including a reduction in allowable exposure levels. Genetic monitoring is performed to reduce or eliminate health risk resulting from genetic damage.

Genetic monitoring may hold less threat of employment discrimination than genetic screening, because such monitoring is conducted to determine relationships among hazardous materials, genetic changes, and any subsequent disease processes. Research on the survivors of Hiroshima and Nagasaki demonstrated long delays in the appearance of illness. "Although genetic changes such as chromosomal damage have been associated with exposure to radiation and some chemical mutagens or carcinogens, little is known about which changes are predictive of subsequent disease risk," says a report by four federal agencies (Department of Labor et al. 1998, p. 3).

Genetic Information and Workplace Discrimination

There are several ways in which genetic information can make its way into employment decisions through medical records, some not requiring genetic testing. When employees give family medical histories or make comments during physical examinations, health history data may be recorded that allows physicians to make inferences about possible genetic illness. Another source of such information is the laboratory assessment of a person's output of specific chemical substances, where certain patterns in the results of such tests may suggest genetic characteristics. However, the most direct approach is through an analysis of a person's genetic material, the DNA. This genetic material may reveal indicators of an existing disease, a disease that may develop later in life, or the prospect of having a child with a hereditary illness.

The Sickle Cell Example

In the early 1970s employers used genetic screening to identify carriers of the mutated gene for sickle cell anemia among their African American employees. Even though a cure for sickle cell anemia was not available, federal and state legislation was passed between 1970 and 1972 requiring mandatory screening for African American citizens. While much has been written about this example of genetic screening (Reilly 1975, 1977), three major criticisms have been identified (Markel 1992). First, the screening programs had a racial problem, given that they were applied exclusively to African Americans, even though other groups, such as people of Mediterranean origins, can be carriers. Second, these laws were often characterized by scientific inaccuracy, especially with respect to the way they seemed to equate "carrier status" with "disease status," having the effect of stigmatizing carriers. Third, in their haste to create these laws, legislators omitted several important protective clauses, such as requiring test result confidentiality.

Some companies did learn valuable lessons from their experience with screening for sickle cell anemia. DuPont found itself in hot water with charges from a national newspaper stemming from offering employees the option to refuse the test (Dutton

1995). After the controversy, DuPont changed its policy, giving employees the option to request the test.

Fear of Discrimination

Unfortunately, examples of discrimination and stigmatization related to genetic testing are not limited to the case of sickle cell anemia. Geller (1996) reports on a survey of persons associated with genetic conditions that revealed more than 200 cases of genetic discrimination among the 917 respondents. The surveyed populations contained parents of children with genetic conditions and people at risk of developing such conditions, and about 22 percent reported discrimination by employers, insurance companies, and other organizations using genetic information.

Such negative experiences are consistent with the fears of adverse consequences of genetic testing reported in a number of recent surveys.

1. Many of these were summarized in a government agency report (Department of Labor et al. 1998) that reviewed findings of high percentages of respondents who reported a reluctance to use genetic testing because they feared that the results would be used to justify the denial of jobs or access to health insurance policies.

2. Frieden (1991) cites an interview with Paul Billings in which he revealed having received 40 responses to an ad in the *American Journal of Human Genetics* that asked people to contact him about cases of genetic discrimination.

3. Eighty-five percent of respondents in a 1995 Harris Poll indicated that they were either very or somewhat concerned about the access and use of genetic information by insurers or employers (Department of Labor et al. 1998).

4. Lapham, Kozma, and Weiss (1996) reported that 17 percent of a sample of 332 members of support groups for families with genetic disorders did not reveal genetic information to employers out of fear of discrimination.

5. In a 1997 national telephone survey by the National Center for Genome Resources, 63 percent of more than 1,000 respondents "would not take genetic tests" if employers and health insurance organizations could gain access to the results. Eighty-five percent "felt that employers should be prohibited from obtaining information about an individual's genetic conditions, risks, and predispositions."

6. Kolata (1997) reports that approximately one-third of a sample of women who were at high risk for breast cancer because of gene mutations refused to participate in a study concerned with keeping them healthy because they feared discrimination or loss of privacy.

These studies and data from individual cases (Frieden 1991; Geller 1996), support the idea that Americans do fear adverse consequences from the disclosure of genetic information to employers and insurers, and that these fears are not groundless. Furthermore, it is not comforting to learn that the reason that insurers, HMOs, and employers do not plan to utilize genetic screening is the issue of costs (Frieden

1991). They do not indicate that they will not use such information if they acquire it in a less expensive manner. In fact, says Frieden, "cases of alleged genetic discrimination by insurers stem mostly from insurance companies getting access to results of tests already taken, rather than making their own tests on suspicious applicants and awaiting the results" (Frieden 1991, p. 44). Americans are left with yet another example of "don't ask, don't tell."

Restricting the Use of Genetic Information in the Workplace

The primary justification of using genetic information in employment situations would be empirical evidence of an association between an individual's unexpressed genetic factors and his or her job performance. Because no such evidence exists, most authoritative groups are correct in recommending either a prohibition or a severe restriction on the use of genetic testing and genetic information in the workplace. Two major panels of health care authorities have recently taken such a position.

In an editorial in the *Journal of the American Medical Association* on genetic testing by employers, the Council on Ethical and Judicial Affairs (1991) of the American Medical Association expressed a two-part opinion. The Council stated, "It would generally be inappropriate to exclude workers with genetic risks of disease from the workplace because of their risk" (p. 1830). Genetic testing, it said, lacks sufficient predictive power and would result in unfair discrimination against those with abnormal test results. Furthermore, better means of predicting employee performance are available. However, periodic monitoring of workers exposed to dangerous substances is justified as a means of protecting those individuals who may have greater genetic susceptibility to such agents. The Council concluded, "There may be a very limited role for genetic testing in the exclusion from the workplace of workers who have a genetic susceptibility to occupational illness." It offered a set of conditions that would have to be met to allow such a form of genetic testing.

Members of the Committee on Genetic Information and the Workplace of the National Action Plan on Breast Cancer (NAPBC) and the National Institutes of Health-Department of Energy Working Group on Ethical, Legal, and Social Implications of Human Genome Research (the ELSI Working Group) have published a set of five recommendations for state and federal policymakers regarding discrimination and privacy concerns in the workplace (Rothenberg et al. 1997). These authors also note that although employer-required genetic tests are typically not prohibited, "there is insufficient evidence to justify the use of any existing test for genetic susceptibility as a basis for employment decisions" (p. 1755). They said that even if genetic testing is not used, employers can obtain such information through other means and demonstrate a reluctance to hire or promote those persons whose disease may interfere with work in the future or may cause benefits cost to escalate. Therefore, they urge state and federal policymakers to prohibit employment organizations from using, requesting, or requiring the collection of genetic information. Rothenberg et al. (1997) also want to restrict employer access to genetic information in medical records and to prohibit the disclosure of such information by employers without written authorization. Finally, they urge that strong enforcement mechanisms be applied to violators.

Similarly, The American Society of Human Genetics has issued a statement on genetic testing for breast and ovarian cancer predisposition (American Society of Human Genetics 1994) recommending against mass screening for BRCA1 mutations that are believed to be responsible for about 5 percent of breast cancer cases. The rationale for not engaging in mass screening is based on three practical issues: the probability that a given mutation will result in cancer, the effectiveness and risk of available interventions, and test reliability. Unfortunately, this group's statement is not as clear about direct workplace issues as are the statements by other groups cited above.

Legislative Protection

Even though President Clinton announced that he would support legislation and regulation to protect employees from genetic-based discrimination (Shogren 1998), progress in this area has been slow. The Genetic Privacy and Nondiscrimination Act of 1997 (Colby 1998) would have provided several forms of direct protection, but it has not passed. It's latest version, The Genetic Privacy and Nondiscrimination Act of 1999 has also not passed. Existing protection comes from other laws and regulations at both the federal and state levels, of which most were not written to directly influence genetic testing. In fact, the few federal-level protections that exist result from laws designed to remedy other types of workplace discrimination. These incidental federal protections are limited in scope and not well-established. Clearly they do not provide American citizens with sufficient protection for the abuse of genetic information for discrimination in the workplace. While state legislative bodies have responded to this vacuum, the legislation they have enacted varies in coverage, specific protections, and approaches to enforcement. Given that the largest employers are most likely to utilize genetic information, and given the differences among state laws, federal legislation to provide consistency across all state boundaries is imperative.

Existing Federal Laws

A single federal law directly addresses genetic discrimination: the Health Insurance Portability and Accountability Act (HIPAA) of 1996. As described in the government agencies' report, "HIPAA prohibits group health plans from using any health-related factor, including genetic information, as the basis for denying or limiting eligibility for coverage or for charging an individual more for coverage" (Department of Labor et al. 1998, p. 9). There has also been close collaboration between the Clinton administration and Congress on legislation to prevent disclosure of genetic information or the use of genetic information in the modification of rates by insurance companies. Both HR 2457 and 5132 have been sent to a house subcommittee and senate committee, respectively. However, many of the problems that may arise from the collection or use of genetic information in the workplace are beyond these issues of health insurance.

A better existing source of protection from discrimination based on genetic information are those laws that prohibit discrimination based on disability. While they do not explicitly address genetic information, the Americans with Disabilities Act (ADA) and other laws prohibiting disability-based discrimination, such as the Rehabilitation Act of 1973, offer some protection against discrimination involving genetic-based disability. The ADA offers protection to individuals whose genetic-based disability is symptomatic. However, it does not offer protection from genetic discrimination to those individuals with an unexpressed genetic condition. Genetic testing may reveal a condition in a person that may not express itself for more than a decade, and the ADA leaves such a person vulnerable to genetic discrimination without penalty.

Those who have a genetic disability that is currently asymptomatic lack established protection against discrimination based on genetic information. People who fall into this category include carriers of a disease who may never express the disease, people who have late onset genetic disorders who are identified through genetic screening as being at high risk of developing the illness, and people for whom family history indicates a high probability of presenting the symptoms.

The Equal Employment Opportunity Commission (1995) has developed compliance guidelines that seek to extend ADA protection to such individuals with asymptomatic genetic disorders. These guidelines advise that "an employer who takes adverse action against an individual on the basis of genetic information related to illness, disease, or other disorders regards that individual as having a disability within the meaning of the ADA" (Department of Labor et al. 1998). The ADA prohibits discrimination against a person with a disability, but this EEOC guidance has a limited scope and legal impact. It is less legally binding in court than a law or regulation and is yet to be tested in court.

The ADA does not ensure the privacy of genetic information because it offers no protection for employees from employer requirements or requests to provide genetic information. The ADA generally denies access by employers to the medical records of applicants before a conditional offer of employment. However, during the interval between the conditional offer of employment and the first day of work, the employer may acquire extensive medical information, including genetic information. During this period, the ADA would not prohibit the employer from requiring genetic screening as a condition of employment or from obtaining genetic information from a specialized data bank. Furthermore, after hiring an applicant an employer may request further medical information so long as it is job-related and necessary for conducting business.

Preventing discrimination based on genetic information is difficult. It is difficult to detect such discrimination because it may be based on indicators of disease risk rather than on the manifestation of symptoms. The employer could have a greater awareness of such risk factors than the employee. Under these circumstances, genetic information could be used to deny employment or promotion without regard to job performance or ability. The rapid progress of the research associated with the Human Genome Project increases the probability that genetic data that appear relatively innocuous today may with future research be found to indicate genetic risk. The threat of such research extends to the civil rights of family members because such information may be used to predict their risk of genetic disease for them, presenting the possibility of large-scale discrimination against future generations.

Additional federal law protection against some forms of discrimination based on genetic information is Title VII of the Civil Rights Act of 1964 (Department of Labor et al. 1998). The link to Title VII derives from those cases where racially or ethnically linked genetic disorders serve as the basis for genetic discrimination, making those cases illegal discrimination based on race or ethnicity. Such protection under Title VII would apply only to cases of discrimination where there is an established link between the genetic trait and the particular racial or ethnic group. Such links have been established for few diseases, and therefore Title VII will serve as an effective tool for very few forms of genetic discrimination. Title VII and the other existing federal statutes and regulations offer a less than adequate response to the threat of genetic-based employment discrimination.

State Antidiscrimination Laws

A number of states have passed legislation to regulate the use of genetic information. Arizona, for instance, enacted a detailed genetic testing act in 1997 that applies to both insurance and employer-worker relations in the workplace. The new law amended the Arizona Civil Rights Act making "it an unlawful employment practice for an employer to fail or refuse to hire, to discharge, or to otherwise discriminate against any individual based on the results of a genetic test received by an employer" (Lewis and Roca 1997).

Conclusions

If the health of American citizens is to benefit fully from the knowledge gained from genetic research, it is important that we eliminate the threat of genetic-based discrimination in employment and insurance decisions. The rudimentary research that has been conducted in this area indicates that the threat of discrimination will lead many people to avoid the tests and treatments that have the potential to benefit their health because they perceive the risk of loss as greater than the potential for gain. Federal legislation should be used to ensure that all Americans have a minimum level of protection from genetic-based discrimination. In providing such protection, such laws will eliminate any conflict with the ability of scientists to conduct research related to genetics and health, especially studies investigating occupational health.

Federal legislation designed to satisfy the twin criteria of ensuring that (1) the discoveries from the Human Genome Project are used to promote health and (2) such discoveries are not used to discriminate against either employees or family members should include these three basic protections (Department of Labor et al. 1998):

1. **Condition of employment or benefits.** Employers will not be allowed to request or require genetic tests or disclosure of genetic information from either potential employees or current employees as a prerequisite for either employment or benefits.

2. Deprivation of employment opportunities. Employers will not be allowed to deny any employment opportunities on the basis of genetic information.

3. Obtaining or disclosing genetic information. Employers will not be allowed to obtain or disclose employee genetic information.

There are, however, circumstances under which the use of genetic testing and genetic information may be necessary to ensure health and safety in the workplace or to allow important research. In those circumstances where an employer is in possession of genetic information about employees, such information must be kept in confidential medical files separate from other human resource records. Federal and state laws should reinforce such a critical information firewall.

The circumstances under which employers should be empowered to gather and store such genetic information would include those cases where it would be important to monitor the effects of exposure to a particular agent on genetic damage, or where the employer is a reasonable choice to become involved in the gathering and storing of data for a genetics research project.

The Department of Labor has argued that such restrictions on the collection, dissemination, and use of genetic information in the workplace should apply broadly to employers, both public and private, and labor unions, as well as to other entities created to influence employment and training, including employment agencies, licensing agencies, and certifying institutions.

Provisions should be made for individuals who have experienced genetic information-based discrimination to file complaints with specific existing federal agencies such as the Equal Employment Opportunity Commission or the Department of Labor. If such designated agencies are not able to effect a resolution of such complaints, the new laws and regulations should empower the agencies to file suit on behalf of the complainants in federal court. The courts should be granted the authority to order appropriate relief for the individual complainant, as already provided in similar civil rights laws. Alternative relief should be available through private civil lawsuit. It is important that the agencies charged with the enforcement of such laws be provided with additional resources for the required investigation and enforcement.

Until the appropriate laws and regulations are in place, the potential promise of the Human Genome Project will remain an ominous threat for those concerned about adverse impact in employment and benefits availability. The creation of the appropriate laws and regulations will facilitate the effective application of genetic information for the rapid improvement of public health.

Recommended Actions

The following points are critical in understanding the issues surrounding genetic testing:

- Genetic testing presents a double-edged sword: the potential for better understanding, detection, prevention, and treatment of genetic based disease versus a new threat of discrimination in the workplace.

- Racial and ethnic discrimination may result because genetic traits that lead to disease are unevenly distributed among racial and ethnic groups.
- Employers and insurance carriers could use genetic information to reduce healthcare costs by excluding those found to have genetic potential for disease.
- Genetic tests lack predictive power for the development of symptoms.
- There is no established link between genetic factors and job performance.
- Genetic screening is used to detect existing conditions or vulnerability, while genetic monitoring involves repeated testing to determine if genetic material has changed as a result of repeated exposure to hazardous substances.
- Researchers have found that more that 20 percent of respondents with genetic conditions have reported workplace discrimination.
- Surveys have shown that approximately 85 percent of respondents have some level of opposition to employer access to genetic information.
- Current federal laws and regulations provide limited and indirect protection against discrimination, applying primarily to those who exhibit symptoms.
- State laws constitute an uneven patchwork of coverage, making it imperative that new federal legislation be enacted to provide consistency.

References

American Society of Human Genetics. "Statement of the American Society of Human Genetics on Genetic Testing for Breast and Ovarian Cancer Predisposition." *American Journal of Human Genetics*, 55(5) (1994): i–iv.

Asch, D. A.; Patton, J. P; Hershey, J. C.; and Mennuti, M. T. "Reporting the results of cystic cibrosis carrier screening." *American Journal of Obstetrics and Gynecology*, 168(1) (1993): 1–6.

Colby, J. A. "An analysis of genetic discrimination legislation proposed by the 105th Congress." *American Journal of Law & Medicine* 24 (1998): 444–453.

Council on Ethical and Judicial Affairs, American Medical Association. "Use of genetic testing by employers." *JAMA—The Journal of the American Medical Association* 266 (13) (1991): 1827–1830.

Department of Labor, Department of Health and Human Services, Equal Employment Opportunity Commission, and Department of Justice. "Genetic information and the workplace." (1998). [on-line]. Available at http://www.dol.gov/dol/_sec/public/media/reports/genetics.htm.

Dutton, G. "If the genes fit (genetic testing and employers and insurance firms)." *Management Review* 84 (10) (1995): 25–29.

Equal Employment Opportunity Commission. *Compliance Manual 2*, Section 902, Order 915.002, 902–45 1995.

Frieden, J. "Genetic testing: What will it mean for health insurance." *Business & Health* 9 (3) (1991): 40–46.

Geller, L. "Individual, family and societal dimensions of genetic discrimination: A case study analysis." *Science and Engineering Ethics 2* (1) (1996): 71–88.

Harper, P. S. "Huntington disease and the abuse of genetics." *American Journal of Human Genetics*, 50(3) (1992): 460–464.

Kolata, G. "Advent of testing for breast cancer genes leads to fears of disclosure and discrimination." *New York Times* 4 January 1997, p. C1.

Lapham, E. V.; Kozma, C.; and Weiss, J. O. "Genetic discrimination: Perspectives of consumers." *Science* 274(5287) (1996): 621–624.

Lewis and Roca, LLP. *Arizona Employment Law Letter* 4 (3) (1997).

Markel, H. "The stigma of disease: Implications of genetic screening." *American Journal of Medicine* 93 (1992): 209–215.

Reilly P. "State supported mass genetic screening programs." In *Genetics and the Law I*. Edited by A. Milunsky and G. J. Annas. New York: Plenum Press, 1975.

Reilly P. *Genetics, Law and Social Policy*. Cambridge: Harvard University Press, 1977.

Rothenberg, K.; Fuller, B.; Rothstein, M.; Duster, T.; Kahn, M. J. E.; Cunningham, R.; Fine, B.; Hudson, K.; King, M.; Murphy, P.: Swergold, G.; and Collins, F. "Genetic information and the workplace: Legislative approaches and policy challenges." *Science* 275(5307) (1997): 1755–1757.

Shogren, E. "Clinton would protect workers from genetic-testing bias." *Nation and World*. 1998 [on-line]. Available at http://www.seattletimes.com/news/nationworld/html98/gene_012098.html.

WORKFORCE CHALLENGES FOR THE TWENTY-FIRST CENTURY

Cornelia G. Gamlem
Workplace Diversity Committee

As we enter the twenty-first century, we see increasing changes within the American workforce. The industrial revolution of the late nineteenth and early twentieth centuries dramatically changed the way people work, with the movement of the workforce from the farm to the factory. This change gave rise to a plethora of laws and regulations designed to redress abuses in the labor market such as use of child labor, lack of protection against injury, layoff for old age and disability, and systemic discrimination against groups of individuals (Anthony, Perrewe, and Kacmar 1999). With the movement now under way from the industrial to the information age, the challenges to human resource professionals increase.

During the early 1960s, the issue of employment discrimination moved to the forefront. While policymakers were beginning to debate models to redress discrimination in employment, racial unrest was giving rise to the civil rights movement. Federal civil rights laws designed to eliminate discrimination resulted. Title VII of the Civil Rights Act of 1964 required most companies and labor unions to grant equal employment opportunity for all. It established the Equal Employment Opportunity Commission (EEOC) to ensure the achievements of Title VII's objectives. Next came Executive Order 11246, in 1965, which prohibited employment discrimination by any employer that has a major contract with the federal government. The Labor Department's Office of Federal Contract Compliance Programs (OFCCP) enforces EO 11246.

Thirty-five years after President Lyndon Johnson signed EO 11246, the use of affirmative action to achieve equal opportunity objectives is still widely debated, particularly in the media. The recent debate has failed to accurately describe affirmative action in the employment context and often confuses it with diversity initiatives. At the same time, there is a growing trend by lawmakers and policymakers to effect social changes via legal and regulatory vehicles rather than by voluntary corporate efforts. For the human resource practitioner, it is important to understand the distinction between federally mandated programs such as affirmative action, and voluntary initiatives to address rapidly changing workforces. This chapter will explain these distinctions and discuss social trends that will affect workplace diversity in the next ten years.

Affirmative action in employment primarily affects companies that receive contracts from the federal government. They are required to comply with the regulations promulgated under Executive Order 11246, the Rehabilitation Act of 1973, and the Vietnam Era Veterans Readjustment Assistance Act of 1974. These laws extend the protections of Title VII to prohibit discrimination and require contractors to exercise outreach efforts so that protected classes have the opportunity to be hired and advance in employment without regard to their race, color, religion, sex, national origin, disability, or veteran status. Rather than providing employment preferences, affirmative action requires companies to actively recruit, interview, and seriously consider a wider variety of candidates. Affirmative action also requires companies to implement policies and programs to help minorities and women advance in employment in those areas of a company's workforce where those groups are not fully represented. Its intention is to remove barriers to employment opportunities and to provide equal employment opportunity for all individuals, not to establish hiring quotas for protected groups. In addition, courts can order companies to establish affirmative action programs to remedy the effects of past discrimination.

In 1987 the Hudson Institute published a study for the Department of Labor entitled *Workforce 2000*. The study reported on workforce changes projected from 1985 to 2000, and documented a shift in labor force demographics with growth in ethnic, racial, and gender groupings (Baytos 1995). These changes would affect not only the workplace, but also external issues such as the changing face of consumers. Demographics were not the only changes affecting companies. Increased competition and entry into global markets were adding demands and pressures. Companies began using a variety of approaches to tap the talent and effectiveness of their workforces, such as high-performance work teams. Important to the success of these teams is the ability of each member to make quality contributions. Companies realized that to be effective they had to manage the diversity of these teams without impeding productivity (Baytos 1995). Driven by these changes, rather than by the legal and regulatory requirements of affirmative action, companies began to implement initiatives that addressed the many dimensions of diversity within their organizations.

Somewhere in the recent debate, the distinction between affirmative action and diversity became blurred and the terms were interchanged, leading to the notion that diversity initiatives are merely affirmative action efforts with a different name. However, if we observe the events along a continuum (see figure 1), society has moved from the golden rule of equal employment opportunity (treating everyone equally as a potential employee), to righting past wrongs that affirmative action is designed to address. Incorporated into affirmative action is the golden rule of equal employment opportunity (EEO) and the principle of nondiscrimination. Moving along the continuum, initiatives have further evolved to emphasize the importance of valuing differences and the importance of including all employees in the workforce, namely workplace diversity. While encompassing the principles of EEO and affirmative action, diversity has a broader reach. Comparing and contrasting these approaches to workplace policies, we see a number of similarities and differences. EEO and affirmative action are constrained by the boundaries of laws and regulations and have a specific mandate, namely, the prohibition of discrimination against defined, protected classes. While EEO offers no guidelines for correcting past discriminatory practices, affirmative action mandates certain efforts to overcome the effects of past practices. Workplace diversity initiatives are not rooted in laws and regulations. They have no defined responsibilities and no constraints. Therefore, they can be broadly defined to address specific issues within a company. While EEO and affirmative action are rigid, workplace diversity is flexible. The point at which the three intersect, however, represents the common goal that they all share, namely respect (see figure 2).

Figure 1 – Diversity Continuum

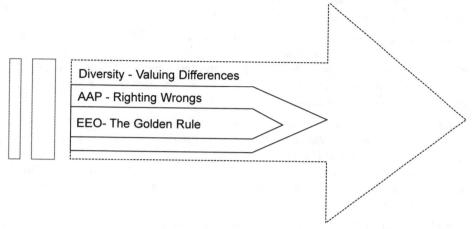

Diversity - Valuing Differences

AAP - Righting Wrongs

EEO- The Golden Rule

Figure 2 – Respect: The Cornerstone

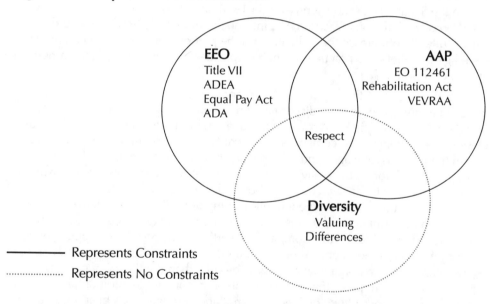

EEO
Title VII
ADEA
Equal Pay Act
ADA

AAP
EO 112461
Rehabilitation Act
VEVRAA

Respect

Diversity
Valuing
Differences

———— Represents Constraints

················ Represents No Constraints

Corporate diversity initiatives address a wide variety of issues that affect the workplace and the marketplace. Workforce diversity can include tenure with the company, the line of business an individual supports, functional specialty, geographic region, and personal aspects such as age, lifestyle, sexual orientation, education, race, and gender. Globalism, and the differences and similarities in terms of people, culture, politics, technology, priorities, and location, are often core issues within a diversity initiative. Acquisitions and mergers provide mixtures of entities that may be different or similar in the nature of the business, corporate culture, vision, mission, and technology. Cross-functional work teams can present a distinct set of diversity issues as companies manage the similarities and differences regarding tasks, goals, communication patterns, and time orientation (Thomas 1996). In order to design effective diversity initiatives, it is important to understand the issues and challenges shaping the workforce and affecting the workplace.

Lawmakers and policymakers remain concerned about discrimination in employment practices. In fact, the trend appears to be toward more protections and entitlements, and to increasing the regulation and reporting requirements imposed on companies, thereby giving the government more oversight of, and impact on, corporate employment practices.

The Veterans Employment Opportunities Act of 1998 expanded the class of veterans protected by the 1974 Vietnam Veterans law. The Act not only expanded the class of veterans who would be protected (e.g., Gulf War veterans), it also imposed additional reporting requirements. Those requirements include reporting not only the new class of veterans, but also reporting on the minimum and maximum number of employees for the reporting year.

The Employment Nondiscrimination Act, which would extend Title VII protection on the basis of a person's sexual orientation, was considered in 1996 but lost by one vote in the Senate. Legislators ignored it in 1998, and it was reintroduced in 1999. The Workplace Religious Freedom Act, introduced during 1998, which would amend Title VII to increase the obligation on the part of employers to accommodate the religious beliefs and practices of their employees, lost momentum after a number of employer groups raised concerns.

In April 1998 the Clinton administration announced the Equal Pay Initiative, designed to address perceived discrimination in corporate pay practices. In early 1999, the Paycheck Fairness Act was introduced in both the House and the Senate. Designed to enhance enforcement of the Equal Pay Act, it prohibits sex discrimination in the payment of wages and imposes uncapped compensatory and punitive damages (in addition to back pay and liquidated damages remedies already available). The Act directs the Secretary of Labor to develop guidelines to compare wage rates for different jobs with the goal of eliminating disparities in pay between men and women performing work that is different in content determined to have equivalent value (comparable worth). Comparable worth is a theory which supports equal pay for jobs that are not identical or are different in content, but that may have equivalent value to the organization. This is broader than the theory of equal pay for equal work, which requires that jobs be identical in content. In addition, the Department of Labor's Office of Federal Compliance Programs has been rigorous in auditing compensation practices of federal contractors.

As we move into the twenty-first century, an understanding of workforce predictions is necessary in order to address the challenges they present. According to Hattiangadi (1998), skilled labor shortages are expected to continue into the future, placing an increased emphasis on recruitment. This will continue the trend of new employment opportunities for a broader, more diverse, group of job-seekers, including women, older individuals, and people with limited skills and experience. Economic theory suggests that as labor markets tighten the economic costs of discrimination rise. Thus, in the early twenty-first century, with demand outpacing supply, employers are looking to recruit from untapped labor pools, increasing employment opportunities for protected groups.

Additionally, Hattiangadi (1998) asserted that Hispanics are expected to be one of the fastest-growing groups in the population. By 2010, this population may become the second largest ethnic/race group. Despite rapid growth, the Hispanic labor force is predicted to grow to 14 percent of the U.S. workforce by 2020. The representation of African Americans in the labor force is expected to remain constant at the current level of 11 percent into the year 2020. Asian/Pacific Islanders are predicted to represent 6 percent of the labor force by 2020.

The workforce of the twenty-first century will differ significantly in its share of older individuals because the age distribution of the population will shift as workers of the baby boom generation age. Demographers predict that by the year 2010, baby boomers will leave the workplace through retirement, taking with them needed skills and experience. Because the next generation is smaller and fertility rates are declining, workers with the requisite skills and experience to replace these retirees will be scarce. Allowing this group of older workers, who will be healthier and more highly educated than the prior generation of retirees, to continue participating in the labor force will be critical (Kindelan 1998).

The most significant change in the workforce over the past 30 years has been in gender composition. The number of women in the workforce has doubled since 1970, and by 2020 the female share of the labor force is predicted to be about 50 percent. While this change represents only a small increase from 46 percent in 1998, women have considerable opportunity to increase their participation in the workforce. Women work part-time more than men and average only 1,290 annual works hours compared with 1,900 for men. Only about 60 percent of the women in the labor force work full-time year round. (Hattiangadi 1998).

While demographics predictions are significant, it is also important to look at the educational attainment of ethnic and racial groups, as well as the role of immigration. Hispanics and African Americans lag behind both whites and Asian/Pacific Islanders with respect to high school diplomas and higher education degrees. Among Hispanics, this results in large part from strong immigration of relatively low-skilled individuals from Mexico. Most immigrants admitted to the United States during 1996 were from North America, with native-born Mexicans composing almost 50 percent, Asians 34 percent, and Europeans only 16 percent. With respect to educational attainment, today's immigration is a bipolar distribution, consisting of people with college or advanced degrees and highly specialized skills (12 percent have graduate or advanced degrees) and people with little education or few skills (Hattiangadi 1998).

The rise in immigration brings other notable changes to the workplace. For example, the number and diversity of languages spoken in the workplace today presents multiple opportunities for miscommunication and misunderstanding. The barriers are more than those of language, however. They encompass cultural, gender, economic class, ethnic, educational, and religious differences. Success for managers often means feeling comfortable in a multicultural work environment and discovering new ways of communicating and managing conflicts. Managing these changes is the role of human resource professionals (Grimsley 1999).

The Islamic religion is expected to surpass Judaism as the second most commonly practiced religion in the United States. Because many of our country's social customs and mores are rooted in Christian-Judeo beliefs, significant social changes can be expected to emerge, and these changes will affect the workplace. Employers will have to accommodate the daily prayers, washing, dietary requirements, holidays, clothing, and grooming that are part of these religions (Minehan 1998). Human resource professionals face the challenge of educating themselves and their employees about different religions and their impact on the workplace.

This chapter began by discussing affirmative action as a social program designed to address civil unrest three decades ago. Affirmative action was originally designed to remove barriers in employment for African Americans. Issues related to race still confront the nation, as was reported by the Advisory Board of President Clinton's Initiative on Race (White House 1998). Attitudes and behaviors, both organizational and individual, continue to create barriers and give unfair advantages. Other kinds of barriers to employment exist as we enter the twenty-first century. Poor language skills and lack of education are limiting employment opportunities for some workers. External pressures such as competition, skilled labor shortages, globalization, and immigration are driving the need for companies to attract, manage, and retain a continually changing workforce. Human resource professionals should lead the effort within their organizations to respond to these challenges for workers and employers alike. They need to recognize that EEO and affirmative action are still viable tools for overcoming barriers that should be incorporated into diversity initiatives.

A tight labor market has made recruiting high-skilled workers a business priority. Creative sourcing of candidates results in innovative outreach programs, the very heart of affirmative action. When the demand for workers outpaces the supply, moving beyond outreach becomes necessary. Affirmative action requires programs that allow employees to advance in employment. Emphasizing programs for training individuals lacking skills is one example. Education as an enhancement to employment advancement will likely result in the growth of partnerships between educational institutions and corporations.

Many social and corporate policies in existence today were designed for workplaces that no longer exist. These rigid policies are a barrier to employment in workplaces that need to be flexible to compete. A number of social initiatives being debated today, while not traditionally thought of as components of affirmative action programs, do address barriers. For example, Social Security reform will affect the role that the older worker will play in the workforce of the future. Employers will want to keep valued older workers on the job by offering alternative working arrangements such as consulting assignments and phased retirement programs (Kindelan 1998). The contingent workforce will continue to grow by choice, providing greater flexibility in the workforce. A 1999 study by the Bureau of Labor Statistics confirms that a large margin of contingent workers prefer their status to traditional, full-time employment (Bureau of Labor Statistics 1998). The greater flexibility that contingent working arrangements provide will be attractive to the older worker. Companies are introducing policies supporting flexible hours and work spaces, and these programs can assist with the retention of working parents, especially mothers, who need help balancing work and family responsibilities. By retaining women within its workforce, a company also supports affirmative action. The range of work/family issues continues to grow, and companies are challenged to address their employees' work/life balance needs and lifestyle differences.

Human resources professionals can be on the cutting edge of social and organizational change. They can influence the challenges discussed in this chapter by raising organizational awareness about the myths and misrepresentations of affirmative action and educating managers that EEO and affirmative action are components of diversity initiatives. Shifting beyond affirmative action to workplace diversity initiatives, organizations can build inclusive workplaces and change cultures to reflect the current social trends. In doing so, organizations can address workplace changes before social changes are imposed through legislation.

For diversity initiatives to be successful, they must be built on the cornerstones of inclusion and respect. Inclusive workplaces promote respect by encouraging effective communication, setting a climate for learning, and removing barriers to employment and to external factors such as customer and investor interests. Fostering respect increases productivity and builds a competitive advantage for the organization. Diversity initiatives must also be integrated into the organization's overall business strategy and not be limited to human resources and people management strategies. Diversity must be woven into all of the organization's components, including marketing, public relations, and investor relations. A well-integrated, skillfully crafted workplace diversity initiative will position organizations to respond to social changes, create richer corporate environments, and meet organizational goals and objectives.

Recommended Actions

- Build your diversity initiative on the cornerstone of inclusion and respect.

- Recognize that your workplace diversity initiative is a process and not an event.

- Ensure that your workplace diversity initiative supports your organization's business goal and is integrated throughout the organization.

- Understand the changing nature of the workforce, and develop programs, strategies, and processes that reflect these changes in your workplace diversity initiative.

- Recognize that the changing nature of the marketplace affects your customers and clients, and address these changes in your workplace diversity initiative.

- Monitor and understand changing legal and regulatory constraints and audit these changes against your workplace diversity initiative to ensure that compliance is maintained.

- Challenge impending government changes that will increase your burden and limit your flexibility to respond to changing workforce and market trends.
- Recognize that equal employment opportunity and affirmative action requirements continue to exist and that they can complement your diversity efforts.
- Partner with schools and outreach agencies to narrow the skills gap and address language barriers.
- Assess the diversity issues within your organization with respect to societal issues such as race, gender, and socioeconomic status, as well as with respect to organizational issues such as line of business, geographic region, or functional specialty.

References

Anthony, W. P.; Perrewe, P. L.; and Kacmar, K. M. *Human Resource Management*. 3d ed. Orlando, Florida: Dryden Press, 1999.

Baytos, L. M. *Designing and Implementing Successful Diversity Programs*. Englewood Cliffs: Prentice-Hall, 1995.

Bureau of Labor Statistics. "Workers in alternative employment arrangements: A second look." 1998. [on-line]. Available at http://www.bls.gov/opub/mir/1998/11/art2full.pdf.

Grimsley, K. D. "The world comes to the American workplace." *Washington Post*, 20 March 1999, p. A12.

Hattiangadi, A.U. "The changing face of the 21st century workforce: Trends in ethnicity, race and gender." Washington, D.C.: Employment Policy Foundation, 1998.

Kindelan, A. "Older workers can alleviate labor shortages." *HR Magazine* 43(10) (1998): 200.

Minehan, M. "Islam's growth affects workplace policies." *HR Magazine* 43(12) (1998): 216.

Thomas, R. R., Jr. *Redefining Diversity*. New York: AMACOM, 1996.

White House Commission on Race. "One America in the 21st century: forging a new Future." 1998. [on-line]. Available at http://www.whitehouse.gov/Initiatives/OneAmerica/cevent.html.

THE CHALLENGE: EMPLOYEES FOR THE FUTURE*

Phyllis G. Hartman
School-to-Work Committee

Current Shortages of Skilled/Knowledgeable Workers

As U.S. business moves into the new millennium, companies are struggling to find workers with skills needed to do today's jobs. It came as no surprise to most businesses when the U.S. Department of Labor (DOL) announced a new twenty-four-year low in the unemployment rate—4.3 percent in December 1998, a figure that was still holding as the twentieth century ended (Bureau of Labor Statistics 1999). Besides not having many workers to choose from in an expanding economy, companies are finding that those who are applying for open positions do not have the skills to do the jobs. Sixty-nine percent of North American businesses surveyed by the William Olsten Center for Workforce Strategies in 1998 were facing a lack of applicants with proper skills, up from 41 percent in 1993 (William Olsten Center 1998).

The lack of skills is not limited to the so-called soft skills required by leaner management groups brought on by the total quality management (TQM) programs and downsizing of the 1990s. A vice president of administration for a Michigan manufacturer was quoted as saying, "We are emphasizing the improvement of supervisors' 'people' skills to improve our retention odds," and at the same time "industry is faced with rapidly changing technologies, and greater demand than supply of unique technical skills" (William Olsten Center 1998, p. 6). In addition, many current workers often do not even possess basic literacy skills. A 1997 study of 4,500 National Association of Manufacturers members revealed that 30 percent of their job applicants had inadequate reading and math skills. Six out of ten applicants also had deficiencies in employability areas such as attendance (Kirrane 1998).

Global capital, production, and markets, instantaneous transfer of information, and mass production of "customized" products are all affecting work and life in the United States. In the past, reliance on more natural resources, capital, technologies, and skills kept the American worker on top. Today, only quickly changing skills will bring that result. Secretaries are now information managers, forklift operators control inventory records, auto mechanics are repairing with computer chips rather than with wrenches.

Projections About Future Needs

The current lack of skilled workers is not likely to improve in the near future. The government is predicting that by 2006, 32 percent of all job openings resulting from growth or replacement will require more than a high school diploma. The DOL's December 1998 figures also predict that of the top ten occupations with the largest job growth, only three (cashiers, retail salespeople, and receptionists/information

---

* The author would like to thank Janet Simon, Steve Saylor, and the members of the School-to-Work Committee for their assistance with this manuscript.

clerks) are likely to be ones where on-the-job training alone might be enough (Yu 1998). These numbers become important in light of the increasing numbers of minority workers, specifically African Americans and Hispanics, who traditionally get less education and represent a disproportionately high percentage of the 1 million high school dropouts (Graham 1997). A 50 percent increase in the number of young minorities available for work (those who will reach age sixteen by 2006) could mean that the United States will face an even greater shortage of skilled workers as the current white, baby boomer age group retires (Yu 1998).

A March 1997 article in *Business Week* acknowledged that as the baby boomer workforce ages, there are limited opportunities for younger workers to obtain higher-level skills because the older employees are still working. When the boomers retire, the country may face the prospect of a "shrinking, less skilled workforce after 2020—a phenomenon that would dampen economic growth." Cummins Engine Company in Columbus, Indiana, was cited as experiencing a 29 percent drop in profits in 1996 in the competitive world of engine manufacturing. This drop raised concerns about standing up to continuing competition with an aging workforce whose skills are not increasing at an adequate rate, coupled with no infusion of younger workers because of a 1993 no-layoff union agreement. The young people in the area are moving out in search of better opportunities elsewhere (Stodghill 1997).

While the number of educated/skilled future workers is in jeopardy, the dependence on the people in any organization, whether it be manufacturing or service-focused, seems to be even greater. The Secretary of Labor for the State of Washington, former Boeing Company director, has said, "Today knowledge has become the only source of sustainable, long-term, competitive advantage, but knowledge can be derived only through the skills of individuals. A primary way we will continue to be competitive in the world economy now and twenty years from now is to ensure we have a highly skilled and motivated workforce" (Gayton 1997, p. 26).

Facts That Make Us Face Reality

Even now, businesses are facing shortages in skilled workers. The demand for even greater skills will continue. Knowledge is power in the world of the future, and with the explosion of the use of computers and the Internet, information and its management are keys to success. The greatest increases in population are in those groups who have not had the opportunity to gain strong educational backgrounds. The highest growth in occupations is predicted in jobs like systems analysts, general managers and top executives, nurses, and teacher aides/educational assistants, all of which require more than a traditional high school education.

Younger workers are less likely to get on-the-job experience because of the large number of baby boomers who will not be retired until 2020. Where will they gain the skills and experience necessary to replace the boomers and keep the future economy stable or growing?

Ever-increasing, rapid change in technology, global competition, and the amount of information people are expected to deal with means that new skills are needed for future workers. How can we deal with these new skill needs that we do not even know about, when we are not coping now? Whose problem is it anyway, and who is going to solve it?

Whose Problem Is It Anyway?

Society is suffering. A 1997 *Wall Street Journal* article reported, "In 1979 a 30-year-old male high school graduate earned the equivalent of about $28,000, expressed in today's dollars. Today (1997), a 30-year-old male high school graduate earns about $21,000" (Graham 1997). The ratio of education to earning has declined. Unemployment is at an all-time low. More people are employed in the United States today than in the past twenty-four years. Their pay levels are much lower, however. The two-wage household is more the norm today. Quality of life has not increased for many, even when opportunity for employment has increased. Crime, poverty, and missed opportunity are still prevalent in a society that is experiencing a healthy economic growth.

There are further dangers for society. Manufacturing jobs are moving off shore at an ever-increasing pace. Lower standards of living in other countries offer employers lower-cost employees. Manufacturing, not service, actually creates wealth within an economy. If the trend continues, and U.S. workers are not prepared to take the higher-level/higher paying jobs or those that require technical literacy skills, the United States may lose its place as a world economic leader.

Employers are struggling with responsibility and accountability. The need to turn a profit dominates the philosophy of many business enterprises. The old workplace of the past that "took care" of the employee is all but gone. The loyal employer finds her/himself held down and unable to respond to quickly changing market needs and trends. On the other hand, assuming that knowledge is the power of the future and that only people can have and apply knowledge, employees are the most important resources. Human resources can hold and apply the knowledge effectively. How does management/business meet the needs of the worker in terms of support and loyalty and still make the fast moves and changes dictated by global competition and changing technology? Companies continue to lose out to global competitors when they need to spend financial resources on retraining people on basic skills. They must pass on the costs of this retraining in the cost of their products.

Educators are finding themselves caught in the middle. Traditionally tied since the 1930s to producing people who could succeed in an industrial setting, they feel they are being asked to abandon their well-defined role without the information or the resources to define a new role. Faced with increasing social ills, changes in the family structure, and decreased funds, they are being asked to solve all of the problems. Teachers are expected to educate about conflict management, environmental dangers and issues, and the dangers of drugs and AIDS; improve team-building and communication skills; provide before and after school care; and oh, by the way, still teach reading, writing, math, and social studies. Businesses, often well-meaning but ill-informed, have tried to intervene in education. Efforts to blame or fix schools have been met by resistance from the educational community. It feels the effects of business pointing the finger of blame while they struggle with a crisis of shrinking financial and human resources.

In a *Wall Street Journal*/NBC News poll in March 1997, fifty-nine percent of adults surveyed said that education was essential to success. In the same poll, fifty-eight percent believed that some essential/fundamental changes are necessary in the education systems (Graham 1997).

A significant difficulty faced by schools is the lack of a clear definition for future skill needs. Businesses can't offer future work skills projections. Everyone is aiming at a moving target. In addition, the structure, processes, and available financial and information resources in education today make it difficult to provide timely responses to changing conditions.

What Is the Answer?

Seeking solutions to the problem is only possible by including all stakeholders. Partnership of business, education, and community, as well as parents and students, holds the greatest potential. The need in the workplace is for employees who have a balanced education. They need not only reading, writing, and math skills, but an interdisciplinary application of all three. "Most real-world problems do not fit neatly within the bounds of any one subject area" (Stern and Rahn 1995, p. 39).

The current approach in most schools, and the one most teachers were educated under, was designed around an age-graded, assembly-line pattern, derived from the factory model of the last century (Stern and Rahn 1995). In the traditional assembly line, people were taught to do one function all day, without thinking, like machines. In today's world, change is the key, and learning how to make decisions, work with teams, and solve problems are the components that separate the worker from the machine.

Only by combining the efforts of the total community can U.S. students prepare to be the workforce of the future. Successful programs throughout the country give testimony to the effectiveness of such an approach. "There is plenty of justification for expanding opportunities for work-based learning" (Stern and Rahn 1995, p. 40). For those programs to be most beneficial, they need to be tied to an interdisciplinary curriculum where academics and occupational content go hand-in-hand. Teachers, both academic and vocational, cannot do this alone. They need the resources, both financial and knowledge-based, that businesses possess. Parents need to support schools in this effort, and taxpayers who are not parents need to become involved, often as subject matter experts who can provide volunteer time and information to educators.

What Is the HR Role?

What is the role of the human resources professional in all of this? HR can become a catalyst, a link between business and the community. The emerging role of the HR professional has been as a strategic force in shaping the business of the future by keeping the balance between workers and the organization. This role is a natural fit in re-creating our school and work connections for the future.

As staffing and training professionals, HR is a customer of the community. HR's stake is in helping to develop a strong supply of individuals who can meet future employment needs. By working with businesses, communities, and schools HR professionals become an even more strategic force in everyone's success.

Helping Business and Education Find Each Other

HR professionals have a unique opportunity to use their communication expertise to reach out to local schools and help them link with the resources available in business. Approaching their organizations as employment professionals, they can justify business's investment of time and equipment in support for schools. As community leaders, they can approach schools with the outstretched hand of partnership as opposed to the closed hand and pointing finger of blame.

Examples of successful programs are many and varied, and they go beyond the traditional work-study programs of the past in which vocational students attended school for half a day and worked in local businesses the other half. In Pueblo, Colorado, fifty-three teachers participated in a summer internship program called "Worksite Experiences for Teachers." The program included an employment selection process, an assessment, a one-week internship or shadowing experience, and a curriculum integration workshop. The teachers reported a better understanding of what their students will be facing upon graduation. As a result, new curriculum programs were set up at the schools. In addition, a shared language was established between the educators and the businesses (School-to-Career Resource Center 1998).

School-based enterprises, where teachers and students team with businesses and higher education to create "laboratory" businesses and community projects, have been established. These programs provide students with experience and opportunities to apply learning. One example is Pennsylvania State University's agricultural extension program. The program gets students in inner-city schools in Pennsylvania involved in planting gardens to beautify their school property and often surrounding vacant lots. The students learn about biology and agriculture, the college service provides the plants/seedlings, and the community benefits from an enhanced environment.

Students in school in Eagle County, Colorado, are engaged in a "fish" venture; they built the building and now raise salmon and trout in an ecological system. This raises about $18,000 a year for the school and encourages students to contribute to the ecology of the region. At the same time, the students are learning about biology, ecology, and business, along with problem-solving, cooperation, and teamwork (School-to-Career Resource Center 1998).

Other programs involve workforce development projects combining business leaders, local governments, and professional associations. An example is the YouthWorks program in Pittsburgh, Pennsylvania. Inner-city high school students are employed for the summer through a partnership of local government, economic development advocates, private businesses, and the Pittsburgh Human Relations

Association. A Lehigh Valley, Pennsylvania, Cityworks program brings together city government, a federally funded Private Industry Council, and the local SHRM chapter for a four-day workforce development program that includes local underemployed and hard-to-employ young people each year.

Still other programs include use of community-accepted skill standards, academic passport, or certification programs, use of high school records as standard hiring documents, and community service built into academic or extra-curricular programs.

There are opponents of school-to-work initiatives. Some claim that efforts to set national standards for education will hurt minorities and disadvantaged kids. Others fear standards that will hurt religion. Some believe that school-to-work means that kids will be buttonholed into low-paying manufacturing or service jobs and not encouraged to go on to higher education (Graham 1997). These fears are often unfounded. For instance, most school-to-work programs are based on strong educational principles of "learner-centered" education (National Center for Research in Vocational Education 1997). It would appear that the real danger here lies in limiting the solution of the problem to the control of only one segment of the community. If business, educators, taxpayers, parents, or students try to solve the problem alone, then the doomsayers' predictions could be realized.

HR professionals have an opportunity to create initiatives and establish links that can lead to successful programs within their communities. Working with their own businesses or local SHRM chapters, they can become recognized leaders in an effort to prepare the future workers. They can:

- Initiate programs.
- Participate as advisers to programs.
- Provide input into school curriculum.
- Recruit other employers to participate.
- Assist in screening student or teacher applicants for programs.
- Create work-based staff development opportunities for teachers.
- Provide work-based learning opportunities for students (Kazis and Gittleman 1995)

As developers of workplace policies, HR professionals can contribute in another way. With the number of working parents increasing and the impact of laws like the Family and Medical Leave Act (FMLA), the HR professional can be proactive in development of family-friendly policies. These policies, which can support workplace attendance while supporting community involvement, can contribute to citizen support of local schools. Policies that allow, even encourage, parents to attend school functions will provide support for schools and educators. They represent an outstretched hand to the value of schools. Policies should not be limited to those that affect parents alone. Encouraging employees to become involved in their local schools through time off or flexible scheduling is an investment in the community and the future workforce. HR professionals can help businesses see these links and the ultimate paybacks.

Where Can HR Professionals Start?

SHRM's School-to-Work Committee is one resource for the HR professional. The committee's program, "Educators and Business—Partnership for a Successful Future," available on-line, provides a PowerPoint/slide and script presentation that will help HR professionals in approaching local schools. The program outlines the challenges, the need for a partnered approach among business, education, and the community, a model for school-to-work initiatives, and guided discussion format (SHRM School-to-Work Committee 1998). The Committee also has a reference manual, available by calling SHRM headquarters at 800-283-7476.

In addition, SHRM's home page contains links to many school-to-work sites. Examples of organizations, resources, successful programs, and contacts can be found there. The Web site address is http://www.shrm.org/committees/stw.

The real key to realizing the potential for school-to-work activities from an HR professional's perspective is acknowledging the critical nature of the efforts of every individual. Preparing the future workforce is not in the hands of any one group or individual. HR professionals can be an important catalyst to these efforts by using their already established understanding of business and strategic planning, and by building partnerships among the community, business, and the profession. Taking a step to make these networks a reality will help HR stand out once again as a strategic force in a successful future.

Recommended Actions

- Initiate school-to-work partnerships in your own community.
- Participate as advisers to existing programs.
- Provide input into school curriculum.
- Assist in screening student or teacher applicants for programs.
- Create work-based staff development opportunities for teachers.
- Provide work-based learning opportunities for students.
- As developers of workplace policies, be proactive in development of family-friendly policies that encourage parent/community involvement in local schools.
- Encourage employees to become involved in their local schools through time off or flexible scheduling as an investment in the community and the future workforce.
- Explore SHRM's school-to-work links through the Web site: http://www.shrm.org/committees/stw.

- Be an important catalyst by using already established understanding of business and strategic planning, and by building partnerships in the community, business, and the HR profession.

References

Bureau of Labor Statistics. Press release. Department of Labor, 1999 [on-line]. Available at http://stats.bls.gov/newsrelease/empsit.toc.htm.

Gayton, C. C. "Getting into the education business." *Techniques* 72(5) (1997): 26–28.

Graham, E. "Education becomes the paramount issue." *Wall Street Journal*, 14 March 1997, p. R4.

Kazis, R., and Gittleman, M. "School-to-work programs." *Info-Line* Issue 9509, (September 1995).

Kirrane, D. E. "Good help is harder to find." *Association Management* 50(3) (March 1998): 33.

National Center for Research in Vocational Education. "School to work for the college bound." *Centerfocus* 16 (March 1997): 1.

School-to-Career Resource Center. "Effective examples in Colorado." August 1998 [on-line]. Available at http://ccdweb.ccd.cccoes.edu/stcresource.

SHRM School-to-Work Committee. *Educators and Business—Partnership for a Successful Future*. 1998 [on-line]. Available at http://www.shrm.org/committees/699stwpost.pdf.

Stern, D. and Rahn, M. "Work-based learning." *Educational Leadership* 52(8) (1995): 37–38.

Stodghill, R. "The coming bottleneck." *Business Week* 35 (49) (1997): 184.

William Olsten Center for Workforce Strategies. *Staffing strategies: 1998 Olsten Forum on Human Resource Issues and Trends*. Melville, New York: William Olsten Center, pp. 1–6.

Yu, J. L. Bureau of Labor Statistics of the Department of Labor. December 1998 [on-line]. Available at http://stats.bls.gov/blshome.html.

Suggested Readings

SHRM School-to-Work Committee. School to work reference manual. Alexandria, Virginia: Society for Human Resource Management, 1999.

School-to-Work Resources. Examples of organizations, resources, successful programs, and contacts. SHRM March 2000 [on-line]. Available at http://www.shrm.org/committees/stw.

PROTECTING A COMPANY'S VALUABLE INTANGIBLE ASSETS IN THE INFORMATION AGE*

Linda S. Johnson
Employment Committee

Whether a company is large or small, chances are pretty high that some form of information is among its most valuable assets. From customer lists to marketing plans, from product formulation to pricing information, data and information are increasingly becoming the commodities of the future. This phenomenon has been coupled with the increased use of technology by businesses to collect, store, and distribute information. As a result, never before have businesses been so vulnerable to unauthorized access to and use of company information. And never before has the need to maintain the confidentiality of such information been as vital to keeping a competitive edge in our fast-paced, rapidly changing global marketplace.

Some companies, especially those in the high technology industry, have wisely recognized the need to protect company information and already require some employees to sign employment agreements that include nondisclosure and noncompetition provisions. Other companies have adopted specific policies governing the use of e-mail or the Internet. But these employment agreements and focused information security policies frequently fall short of providing a company with the full security it should have for protecting itself against inappropriate use or disclosure of important company information. For whatever reason, companies are often lax in uniformly or consistently adopting protective employment agreements. And even when there is an information security policy in place, it typically addresses only a certain technology such as e-mail rather than the information that needs to be protected regardless of the format in which it is maintained.

Why Does a Company Need a Comprehensive Information Security Policy?

The failure to appropriately secure a company's intangible assets can result in numerous problems. The most typical situation involves the employee who leaves his or her employer, goes to work for a competitor, and solicits the customers or vendors of the former employer. Or a company discovers that an ex-employee or soon-to-be ex-employee has deleted software, and that the employee intends to start a competing business to market that software. Sometimes, companies altogether fail to consider that even with current employees, maintaining the security of company information is critical. For instance, certain types of information, such as personnel and employee health records, may carry a legal obligation of confidentiality. Inappropriate disclosure of this information can lead to lawsuits and financial damages. Without proper precautions, anyone with access to company-maintained data (i.e., employees, independent contractors, interns, or even building maintenance or janitorial crews) can discover and download vast amounts of company data with

* The author would like to thank David Wolowitz, Esq., and Sarah B. Knowlton, Esq., for their assistance with this manuscript.

minimal effort. Even office recycling bins can pose a threat to information security if nonshredded documents are recycled without consideration of their content.

As we start into the new century, every company should take the time to evaluate its need to adopt a comprehensive information security policy. By doing so, any business that expends significant resources in developing its customer lists, specialized software, unique marketing strategies, and the like will help to ensure that these valuable intangible assets are protected to the greatest extent possible from abuse, both from its existing workforce and from departed employees.

What Should a Company Do First?

The starting point for developing an effective information security system is to create an information security team or committee whose task it is to develop a draft information security policy. The policy itself will have two main components: a statement of general principles and a listing of the means by which the general goals will be achieved. How the team is constituted will be critical to determining the likelihood of its success. Most organizations, especially larger ones, are composed of various constituencies. Successful implementation of a comprehensive information security policy will require acceptance by all of the key constituencies.

No system will succeed without the support of management. Therefore, management must be involved with the drafting of the information security policy from the outset. If the organization is large enough to have an information systems department, the team should include a member of the department. It should also include a member of the human resource department. Selection of other team members will depend on the nature and the makeup of the organization.

The first step, for the team developing the information security policy, is to conduct an audit of all the ways in which information flows into and out of the company. The purpose of the audit is to determine the company's vulnerability to accidental or intentional access or disclosure, as well as to identify the kinds of information developed or maintained by the company. It should evaluate how information is developed, shared, and utilized within the organization. The audit team should find out which documents, if any, are recycled and how the recycled paper is handled. The team should create an audit trail for sensitive computer files so that there is a record of who is accessing company information, and this record should be reviewed periodically. If some levels of employees are not represented on the audit team, the team should involve those employees, asking them to identify areas of concern. With the knowledge it acquires, the audit team can do a risk assessment to determine what weaknesses need to be addressed and what strengths need to be reinforced.

What Should Be Included in the Statement of General Principles?

Following the audit and risk assessment, the information security committee will be ready to prepare its initial draft of the general principles for the information security policy. This statement should include goals, objectives, and responsibilities for information security. The general principles section should be broadly focused so that it will not have to be constantly revised as a result of rapid changes in technology or in how the company itself handles information. It should also be tailored to reflect the ideology and culture of the specific organization.

Although each organization's information security policy will differ, some common elements should be included in any such policy. For example, the policy should clearly state that it governs all information in the company's possession, regardless of the format in which it is maintained. The cornerstone of the policy should be a statement reflecting the fact that the company owns all information within its possession and/or control. Establishing ownership of the information is critical to the company's ability to obtain legal recourse if information is stolen, altered, or inappropriately disclosed. The policy should also clearly define the company's organizational policy for protecting information so that anyone with legitimate access to it understands his or her responsibility as an "information safe-keeper." It should specify who has access to particular information and the purposes for which it can be used. The policy should make clear that employees may not use company information for nonbusiness purposes and may not remove it without authorization. Many companies have failed to implement policies that make clear their proprietary interest in the business information and the technology or systems that support it. A policy that is developed after an employee removes critical information may be too late to protect the company's interests.

An information security policy should define what types of confidential or proprietary information are covered by the policy. While there are already laws, such as state and federal trade secret laws, that generally prevent an employee or other individual from inappropriately using proprietary information of a current or former employer, what qualifies as a trade secret or protectable proprietary information may be open to questions. Such questions can be greatly minimized or even eliminated through the information security policy. For certain types of information such as sensitive computer files, the company will want to limit the people who have access to the information and restrict the opportunity to obtain or duplicate information.

The information security policy should also include procedures for how information should be protected, such as through passwords or lock and key for hard copies, and ensure that these procedures are followed. If a company seeks court assistance in protecting its information, one of the first questions the court will ask is "Did you actually treat the information confidentially?" A court will be less likely to provide the company with a legal remedy if there is evidence that so-called "confidential information" has not been maintained confidentially because of inappropriate disclosures or sloppy or inadequate security procedures.

An information security policy should make clear the need for security and the significance of failure to comply with its requirements. A policy without enforcement will be ineffective. Education and awareness should not be overlooked. The general policy should create a permanent information security team whose responsibility is to maintain awareness of information security issues throughout the organization.

Finally, another common element in the general principles of most information security policies will be a statement that employees do not have an absolute expectation of privacy in information generated in the workplace. It should explain that there may be legitimate business reasons or instances, such as investigations of theft or discrimination, or even as simple a reason as an employee's absence, when the company will need to access an employee's e-mail, voice mail, or other company equipment. It should be clear that the use of technology or any information medium for harassment, or any other inappropriate intrusion, will not be tolerated.

After the draft statement of general principles for an information security policy has been created, the team should submit it to top management for review. It is crucial that management buy into the general goals and objectives of any information security policy before it is implemented. Moreover, before the team can complete the policy by developing procedures and controls relating to specific technologies, events, and behaviors, it needs to know that its general statement of principles is acceptable to management.

An example of the statement of general principles of a comprehensive information security policy follows:

Information and the systems that create, store, and transmit it are critical and sensitive assets of the ABC Company (the "Company") which must be protected. Any information owned by or in the custody of the Company, including personal employee information for which there is an established business, regulatory, or legal need, whether generated internally or received from external sources, is considered the property of the Company. In addition, the Company is the custodian and caretaker of countless pieces of confidential information belonging to and pertaining to our clients and their affairs. This information is often not in the public domain and it is highly sensitive. It has been entrusted to the Company with an expectation that it will be maintained in confidence.

The Company has a responsibility to protect its information and information systems in an appropriate manner from unauthorized or unintended use, disclosure, destruction, alteration, or violation. The security of information must be maintained regardless of how the information is stored (e.g., computer, voice mail, paper). It is the responsibility of every employee and subcontractor to be vigilant in protecting the integrity of Company information and information systems from violation by internal as well as external sources. The degree of sensitivity of information will determine the appropriate level of security to be utilized. Every employee and subcontractor shall acknowledge receipt and review of the Company's information security policy by signing and dating the attached acknowledgment and returning it to the Human Resource Department for inclusion in the employee's personnel file. All references to "employees" herein shall include subcontractors, interns, and any other person who is authorized to be on Company premises for business reasons. New employees or those who have not been trained on information security procedures must receive such training before they access or utilize any Company information. Any incident with respect to a breach of security or concerns about the integrity of information systems should be reported immediately to the Director of Information Systems. Internal security audits will be conducted by the Company from time to time to evaluate the effectiveness and adequacy of security measures.

Information and information systems are intended to be used for Company business. Sending messages that may be considered offensive, harassing, intimidating, or discriminatory is prohibited, as is use of such information or systems for personal gain. Occasional personal use is permitted as long as the use does not affect the Company's productivity or interfere with the Company's business operations. Employees should keep in mind, however, that even personal files and information may be accessed by the Company if there is a legitimate business, regulatory, or legal need for doing so. Any unauthorized use will be considered a misappropriation and may subject the employee to disciplinary action, including dismissal.

Personal codes and devices, such as passwords, alarm codes, keys, access cards, and voice mail identifiers, have been provided to employees to enhance the security of information and systems and to facilitate access to Company premises at times when the building may not be open to the public. These passwords, codes, and devices should never be shared with others, even within the Company. Passwords for all programs should be changed routinely to safeguard the security of the Company's assets, even if the change is not automatically prompted.

Each administrative department within the Company is responsible for identifying security needs that are specific to its operations and functions. Employees in each department will be responsible for familiarity with particular policies that supplement the general security policy.

The foregoing is a statement of the Company's general policy on information security. It applies to all of the Company's employees, subcontractors, information, systems, and technologies, whether or not they are specifically mentioned herein. Upon termination of employment for any reason, each employee will be expected to return any property belonging to the Company, including computer disks, documents, copies, notes and personal identifiers.

How to Achieve the Goals Set Forth in the General Principles

After the information security policy's general principles have been approved by management, the team must shift its focus to developing the procedures and controls necessary to achieve the general goals. It may be wise at this point to alter the makeup of the team to include employees who utilize certain technologies on a daily basis. There are certain systems and technologies that will require more definitive directives for proper security. Among the items that a company should consider having are specific sections on physical files and hard copies of information, facsimile transmissions, laptop computers and disks, Internet and e-mail, telephones and voice mail, computer workstations, and special precautions for telecommuters. These narrower procedures and controls will be more technologically focused and will need to be revised more often than the general goals as technology changes and as problems with the procedures become evident. In addition to sections on specific technologies, some of the specific procedures and controls will focus on events such as hiring and firing. Still others will focus on certain behaviors such as use of technology for personal purposes or sharing of passwords.

Examples of specific technology-based and other types of policies that should be in a comprehensive information security system are the "Internet and E-mail" and "Computer Workstations" sections that follow:

Internet and E-mail

Internal and external e-mail systems are available to employees to assist with the conduct of business. The electronic mail system hardware and software are assets of the Company, as are all messages composed, sent, or received on the e-mail system. Employees should remember that the Company may access e-mail messages for any business, regulatory, or legal purpose.

Each user of the e-mail system has a personal password, which should not be shared and which should be changed frequently to avoid unauthorized access. Even when passwords are properly used, confidentiality of messages should not be assumed. E-mail messages placed in "trash" are retained for a period of sixty days by the Company. Messages not placed in "trash" will be retained indefinitely until deleted by the employee. Each employee should treat each other person's messages as strictly confidential and should not attempt to gain access to someone else's messages without that person's permission.

Caution should be exercised when using external e-mail via the Internet. Although intentional interception of external e-mail is prohibited by law, e-mail over the Internet is not as secure as standard telephone service. Remember that e-mail messages, as any electronically stored data, may be discoverable in litigation. Finally, no information may be posted to a Web site or otherwise disseminated on the Internet on behalf of the Company without the permission of the Executive Director of the Company or the Company's Director of Information Systems.

Computer Workstations

Each employee must have a personal password in order to gain access to the computer network and to certain programs. Passwords must be changed routinely and should be kept strictly confidential. Each user should log out of the system and switch off his or her terminal at the end of the day.

Receptionists and others working in public areas that are visible or accessible to nonemployees should not leave information on the monitor when away from the work station and should utilize password-protected screen savers. During extended breaks or lunch, employees in public areas should log out of the system.

An information security system should also inform employees that their rights to access and use company information terminate when they are no longer employed by the Company. Companies should create a post-termination checklist to ensure that employees return all company property, including copies of all information, before they leave and that computer and other access is terminated on that day. The policy itself should provide penalties for violations so that there is an incentive to comply with the policy. An important precaution is to create and test a disaster recovery plan to recover the information if it is lost, destroyed, or stolen.

How Should a Company Implement the Policy?

Implementation of an Information Security Policy should begin with educating and training employees and others subject to the policy and seeking their input on how to ensure that the policy is followed. Every covered individual, from employees to interns to independent contractors, should be required to sign and date an acknowledgment form stating that the individual understands his or her responsibility to safeguard all company information in accordance with the policy and further understands the ramifications (e.g., discharge or termination) of noncompliance.

In developing and implementing a policy, companies should keep in mind that no set of procedures and controls can ever be complete. No organization will ever be able to fully anticipate every information management problem that might arise. Indeed, the very purpose of having an information security policy—with broad statements of principles supported and monitored by a continuingly operating information security team that emphasizes education and, when necessary, enforcement—is to demonstrate that the company is diligent with regard to the protection of sensitive information. A well-constructed information security policy will provide a good faith defense. In the event of disclosure of confidential information, it will also provide an organization with legal recourse if information has been misappropriated. Policies that focus merely on specific technologies, such as e-mail, faxes, and the Internet, run the very real risk of being perceived as incomplete and therefore inadequate. No company can anticipate every point of vulnerability with regard to access to information. But every company can articulate general policies regarding the need to protect confidential and sensitive information. Every company can educate its employees and maintain awareness. And every company can develop a track record of enforcement to demonstrate that it takes its policies seriously. A company that enacts these measures is much more likely to defend itself successfully in the event of an accidental disclosure or theft of information that it has a fiduciary obligation to protect. Companies that discover that crucial information has been misappropriated will be in a better position to recover it if they have a clear policy that provides evidence of their control and ownership of the information.

We are living in the information age. The way we handle information today is different from the way we handled it even 10 years ago, in large part because of dramatic advances in technology. These advances continue to take new shape, seemingly on a daily basis. The years 2000 and beyond will bring about new ways in which we develop, use, and store the vast quantities of information on which most modern businesses rely. The risks are very high that the old methods for dealing with information storage are grossly inadequate. Despite these risks, few companies have taken the proactive measure of developing a comprehensive information

Developing an Information Security Policy

1. Create an information security team or committee.

- Involvement management.
- Involve a member of the information systems department, if any.
- Involve human resources.
- Select other team members depending on nature and makeup of company.

2. Conduct an audit of all ways in which information flows into and out of the company.

- Evaluate how information is developed, shared, and utilized within the company.
- Find out how documents or computers are recycled or destroyed.
- Involve all levels of employees.

3. Prepare a statement of general principles of the policy.

- Include goals, objectives, and responsibilities for information security.
- Define what types of information are covered and who is covered by policy.
- Explain expectations regarding privacy, security, maintenance, and destruction of information.
- Reflect the ideology and the culture of the organization.
- Submit the statement to management for acceptance.

4. Develop procedures and controls relating to specific technologies and behaviors.

- Include, for example, physical files, facsimiles, laptop computers, Internet and e-mail, telephone, voice mail, computers and telecommuters.
- State possible penalties for noncompliance.

5. Implement the policy.

- Disseminate the policy and require a signed acknowledgment by every employee.
- Educate and train all employees about the policy and its implementation.
- Follow up to keep the policy and training current.

security policy. Instead, many have gone only so far as to implement isolated technology-specific policies such as an e-mail or Internet policy. This simply is not enough. As we move into the twenty-first century, all companies should evaluate their need for implementing a comprehensive information security policy. Only by doing so will companies take the necessary risk management steps for securing their valuable intangible assets to the greatest extent possible. Being proactive is always the best defense.

Recommended Actions

- Create an information security team composed of all levels of employee groups.

- Conduct an information security audit of risk assessment to determine the company's vulnerability to accidental or intentional access or disclosure, as well as to identify the kinds of information developed or maintained by the company.

- Develop a comprehensive information security policy that addresses all forms of company information, including e-mail and Internet, voice mail, paper, or computer.

- Educate and train employees and others subject to the policy regarding its provisions.

- Monitor compliance with the policy. Conduct random security audits.

- Review the policy periodically to ensure that it continues to meet the company's needs and is effective.

Suggested Readings

Behar, R. "Who's reading your mail." Fortune, 3 February 1997, 57–70.

Lewis, P. H. "Threat to computers is often the enemy within." New York Times, 2 March 1998, p. B1.

Remnitz, D. and Breed, R. "Network security audits keep the hackers at bay." National Law Journal, 2 February 1998, pp. C9–10.

Rotenberg, M. The Privacy Law Sourcebook: United States Law, International Law, and Recent Developments. Washington, D.C.: Electronic Privacy Information Center, 1998.

Wood, C. C. Information Security Policies Made Easy. Sausalito, California: Baseline Software, 1996.

Young, L. F., and Christenson, G. A. "Guidelines for company policies on employee privacy in the electronic workplace: a report of sample policies and analysis." Cincinnati, Ohio: Center for Information and Technology and Law, College of Business Administration and College of Law, University of Cincinnati, August 1994.

THE FUTURE OF UNIONS

James A. Laumeyer
Employee and Labor Relations Committee

Ever since the enactment of the National Labor Relations Act in 1935, labor unions have been a powerful influence in the United States. In the decades immediately following World War II, unions effectively bargained the terms and conditions afforded all American workers. They were able to influence the election of sympathetic policymakers who would successfully sponsor favorable legislation and regulations. During most of the twentieth century, labor unions enjoyed, and took advantage of, a position of significant power. At the start of this millennium, however, both the future and the vitality of unions are in question. Contemporary articles present conflicting positions as to whether organized labor is a dinosaur on the verge of extinction or whether it will persevere and evolve in response to changes in the political and cultural environment (Hurd 1998; Rosenthal 1998). At the core of this debate is the decline of union membership, best illustrated by the following graph (Bureau of Labor Statistics 1999).

Union Density, 1930–1997
Membership as Percentage of Payrolls

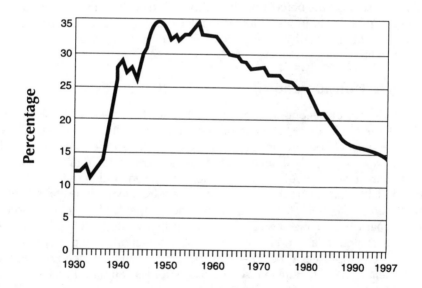

For the human resource professional, the discussion is not theoretical. It represents the basis for previewing human resource jobs in the future. More specifically, the existence of a union in a particular workplace will continue to require additional skills and responsibilities of human resource professionals. Each human resource professional will have a critical role in the determination of the union status of the organization. This chapter provides an accurate projection of labor unions into the next two decades. To understand the current and future status of unions, it is necessary to understand the transformation of unions from a major national power to the current weakened state. Unions do not exist in a vacuum. They have been somewhat decimated by external change forces. The decline is due, in part, to the failure of unions to adjust or adapt, but such contention does not take into account the extent of the forces for change that have dramatically affected labor unions. Further, although unions in general have experienced hardships, unions also have had some successes—for example, significant growth in the public sector and in some specific industries.

This chapter addresses the future of unions in selected industries and workplaces in order to offer insight into the general implications of the winds of change relating to unions. Human resource professionals will recognize the power of personal influence as a primary determinate of the result of union organization efforts in their workplaces. The most appropriate analysis and discussion of the current and future status of unions will not center upon unions themselves, but will focus on the significant forces or drivers of change external to unions. Human resource professionals are fully aware of these significant drivers of change: workforce and employment. Analysis of these drivers is based on statistical information, projections of the data, and the opinion of respected sources. Great care was taken to avoid the trap of simplistic extrapolation. The projections of influential data are represented only by information that has been supported by "expert testimony." Simple extraction certainly would support the perception that labor unions will be nonexistent or meaningless in the near future. But this chapter shows that labor unions will continue to be influential in the future, especially in specific workplaces and under specific conditions.

Workforce Considerations

In today's vigorous economy, many workers have little need for what unions have traditionally offered: competitive compensation, job security, and equitable grievance procedures. Unions continue to tout higher wages for their membership, but surveys show that, in general, higher wages are a lesser concern of workers. Most workers today regard adequate compensation as a given, and this view will continue in the tight labor markets of the early decades of the millennium (Adams 1998). Although some categories of workers do find the prospects of higher pay more attractive, many regard job satisfaction as their primary interest. Unions, however, have demonstrated little or no influence on job satisfaction. Studies have indicated that unionized employees experience less job satisfaction than their nonunion counterparts (Kleiman 1997). Human resource professionals can play a critical role in the delivery of increased job satisfaction to employees.

While unions cannot deliver the workers' premier need, they do have two offerings that are very attractive to certain groups of workers. First is job security (Holley and Jennings 1997). In previous decades, job security was held as sacred only by those employees whose security was threatened. It is ironic that increased numbers of workers are concerned about job security in this tight labor market. Anxiety has increased in the wake of such significant events, such as the passage of the North

American Free Trade Agreement (NAFTA), corporate downsizing, and the growth of outsourcing.

Some concerns of blue-collar workers relating to NAFTA have been justified. The Labor Department reports that more than 210,000 blue-collar jobs (primarily in the manufacturing sector) were lost in the five years after the legislation was enacted. At the same time, NAFTA is reported to have "boosted export-related U.S. economic growth" and created more American jobs (primarily white-collar and service jobs) in a single month than were created in the year before its enactment (Wildavsky 1999). Consequently, Congress will enact new treaties, such as Fast Track, that will have similar results: a loss of blue-collar jobs and a significant gain of other jobs.

Similarly, the concerns of both blue-collar and white-collar workers have been justified relative to downsizing and outsourcing, which have become common strategies for organizations looking for ways to cut costs in highly competitive markets. It has become a common occurrence to find media stories on the corporation that announces the layoffs of thousands of workers. Additionally, the outsourcing of work continues to grow, particularly in the public sector. The Outsourcing Institute in New York "reports that spending on outsourcing has grown fivefold this decade" (the 1990s) (Overman 1997, p. 112). Therefore, it is understandable that workers in search of protection from downsizing and outsourcing will turn to unions. And unions have been responsive to these concerns. Howard A. Sieber, partner and principle consultant for HR Intervention Associates, as cited by Overman, stated:

> Unions work hard to create more language that inserts them into the decision-making process, and they have been successful. I see a resurgence of unions' willingness to exercise strike power to stop, slow or otherwise change management's position, relative to outsourcing or subcontracting (Overman 1997, p. 112).

The second offering used by unions to attract workers builds on employees' strong expectation of fair and respectful treatment. The federal government's propensity for legislating employee rights has reduced the need for unions. But employees still recognize unions as the guardian of fair and respectful treatment in the workplace, and the perception of unfair or disrespectful treatment by management can create an opportunity for a union to organize. The implications for the human resource professional are obvious. Fair treatment of employees is a fundamental objective of human resource management. Therefore, our influence in the positive treatment of employees will aid productivity and retention and perhaps diminish the need for unions in organizations. In his influential study of personnel practices in nonunion companies, Foulkes (1980) found that companies that successfully remained nonunion were more likely to promote management philosophies emphasizing employees as stakeholders and good employee relations. At the level of practice, Foulkes and others (e.g., Fiorito, Lowman, and Nelson 1987) have found that formalized, consistent, and progressive human resource policies substantially reduce employee interest in unionization. According to this analysis, workers' needs will not be the basis for seeking union representation. However, in cases of anxiety over job security or the perception of unfair treatment, groups of employees will seek union representation. The progressive actions of human resource professionals will improve conditions in most organizations, resulting in increased job satisfaction for most workers.

In addition to the worker's wants and needs as cited above, two other conditions positively influence union organization. First, workers tend to favor unions if their companies have a "directive" (chain of command) rather than participative or open culture (Mathis and Jackson 1997). It appears that unionization is perceived as the worker's vehicle for input and participation. This finding is a "call to action" for human resource professionals who perceive that the culture within their companies is directive in nature. While more participative cultures are perceived as conducive to higher productivity, a culture shift can also be justified on the basis of filling this apparent desire of workers to participate. Second, workers who have been union members in the past are more likely to favor union representation (Mathis and Jackson 1997). Accordingly, human resource professionals who work in industries or geographical locations that are heavily unionized should be acutely aware of the inclination. This inclination could have significant implications in the merger of organizations when one or more are organized.

Finally, a very different union leadership is emerging that will create a new appeal to workers. Emergent leaders within labor can be characterized as the "Ivy League Leaders." Highly educated leaders have assumed the helms of labor unions such as the Teamsters, Service Employees, and Hotel Workers. In addition to creating a more "professional image," these leaders are attempting to interest workers in terms of ideology and social issues, in addition to the traditional union offerings. While such offers may not appeal to all workers, it may be very effective in attracting professional workers such as physicians. In essence, this is an evolution of union offerings that has not been fully tested in the workplace until this decade.

Worker Demographics

The demographic profile of the workforce will continue to change dramatically in future decades (Mathis and Jackson 1997). It is very likely that benefit to unions will be slight to moderate. The change in the workforce will continue in the groupings of women and minorities.

Women

It is clear that women will constitute the vast majority of the labor supply for the next two decades. Two out of three applicants for jobs will be female (Mathis and Jackson 1997). Historically, unions have not actively recruited women for membership. Such complaints as the lack of female labor leaders and the lack of sensitivity to women's issues have been common barriers between women and unions in the past. However, the AFL-CIO has now recognized that "Working women absolutely are the future of this labor movement" (Outwater 1997, p. 1).

While not conclusive, studies and surveys have indicated that women are more likely than men to join unions, 49 percent to 40 percent (*Wall Street Journal* 1998). The rationale for the inclination of women to organize is obvious. Though women represent the majority of the workforce, compensation of female workers is collectively lower than that of male workers (Mathis and Jackson 1997). Women continue to dominate low-paying occupations such as clerical jobs and are more likely to work part-time. Women are also likely to be the sole provider for their family. Accordingly, many female workers are more concerned about compensation than the workforce as a whole. Women bring significant needs to the workplace that are unique (Mathis and Jackson 1997)—for example, a greater need to balance family and work demands, and needs for additional flexibility in hours and affordable day care. Often they perceive unions as the vehicle for satisfying these needs.

These inclinations of the largest group of tomorrow's workers should be encouraging for unions. Unions will have a greater opportunity to organize female workers, provided that women find unions more appealing than in the past. Because of the feminization of the workforce and the expressed inclination of women to join unions, human resource professionals should ensure that the needs and preferences of women are addressed within their organizations. By avoiding conditions such as poor treatment or the failure to listen to women, organizations can effectively eliminate the impetus for female employees to seek unionization.

Minorities

Similarly, studies indicate that African American workers have more favorable attitudes toward unions than white workers do. Further, African American workers have a higher percentage of union members (17.7 percent) than white members (13.5 percent) do. While African American workers will not represent a large percentage of the future workforce, this inclination has significant implications for unions and for organizations in many urban areas in this country (Amber 1999).

It is clear that Hispanic workers will constitute a growing percentage of the future U.S. labor force, especially in the Southwest. Attitudes of Hispanic workers have been less favorable toward unions. Hispanics represent the lowest percentage (11.9 percent) of union membership in terms of racial categories. Hispanic females have the lowest percentage (10.8 percent) of union membership (Amber 1999). This is not to say that human resource professionals should consider nonunion status as a given if their workforce is predominantly Hispanic. Progressive human resource practices will still be the most effective factor in workers' consideration of the need for a union in their workplace.

Contingent Workers

One of the fastest-growing sections of the labor force is the contingent worker. Approximately 20 percent of today's workers are parttime or temporary. Because of the nature of their employment, few temporary workers belong to a union (Bureau of Labor Statistics 1984, 1998). Only 7 percent of parttime workers are union members. One of the temporary employment firms is currently the largest employer in the United States, yet unions have not been able to represent this large group of workers. The transient nature of temporary positions is not consistent with traditional union representation; in the private sector there are actually legal barriers to the unionization of temporary workers. While unions have been able to organize large numbers of parttime workers in huge organizations (e.g., United Parcel Service), unions have not been able, presumably for logistical reasons, to organize the vast majority of these workers in smaller organizations. Therefore, it appears that this large group of workers will continue to be nonunion members in the future. Unions appear to have a major misunderstanding of the plight of the contingent workers. Unions characterize contingent workers as victims, or workers trapped in the undesirable fate of a contingent worker. Yet analysis of the composition of these workers indicates that contingent work is a choice, predicated upon personal reasons. More specifically, many of these workers are students, working mothers, or workers between more permanent employment. The demographics of the future workforce provide some encouragement to unions. Clearly, female and black workers have more favorable attitudes toward unions than the white, male workers who have represented the majority of the workforce in the past. The apparent challenge to the human resource profession will be consideration of the sensitive and responsive needs of a diverse workforce.

Private Sector

The private sector has historically been the strength of the labor movement. In the future, however, most unions in the private sector will fight for survival. Much of this twist of fate is a result of the external winds of change and the evolution of the U.S. economy. The most significant changes have been the changes in the nature and the geographical locations of U.S. jobs. These changes have a significant adverse impact on the traditional core unions of the labor movement, and they account for the declining numbers in union membership. These impacts are most noticeable in the analysis of major industries.

Manufacturing

Manufacturing represents the largest occupational group of private sector union members, at 3.2 million members (Bureau of Labor Statistics 1996). Manufacturing jobs continue to be jobs that will be exported as a result of U.S. trade agreements and global competition. Although many manufacturing jobs will be created, the majority will be created in states that have low union membership. For example, *Time* magazine has reported that Arizona and Texas are the "hottest places" for manufacturing jobs in the future (Greenwald 1997). Both of these states have low union membership rates (7% and 6%) (Bureau of National Affairs 1999a) and will not be fertile ground for unionization in the future.

While the outlook for labor is adversely affected by the relocation of a large number of jobs essentially out of unions, there is the potential for unions to replace some lost manufacturing jobs. According to Philip Simon (1999), small companies are now dominating the manufacturing industry. This change is encouraging to unions for two primary reasons. First, unions have demonstrated a higher success rate in organizing small organizations. Second, small organizations do not usually have a full-time human resource professional to ensure the proper treatment of employees and to counsel the company during the organizing activities.

Another potential for union organization relates to industry efforts to streamline processes for purposes of efficiencies. Many large manufacturing companies are consolidating supply, service, and distribution centers. These efforts generally accomplish the stated objective of efficiencies. But some employees may be disgruntled with the company about the consolidation efforts if they have been forced to relocate or to accept jobs that are lower-paying or not to their liking. Therefore, one result of these consolidations is to increase the likelihood of union organizing. In fact, some of these centers have become bigger targets for union organizing. They create the possibility of gaining a large number of new members. Human resource directors in these companies should make every effort to address these issues throughout the planning and implementation of such efforts. These efforts could decrease the chances of union organization.

It is apparent that unions will experience significant losses in membership as a result of the geographical location or relocation of manufacturing jobs in the future. It is also apparent that unions will have more opportunity to add some members in small businesses. It is probable that there will be fewer unionized manufacturing workers in the future and that manufacturing will not be the industry of the greatest union numbers.

Services

The services industry employs the most workers (30.7 million) in the country and represents one of the lowest rates of union membership (5.4%), 1.6 million (Bureau of Labor Statistics 1999b). In general, unions have had very little success in organizing service workers. There are several factors that could assist unions in their organizing efforts. First, it is possible, but unlikely, that Congress will legislate single-site bargaining units. Because most service companies are small and comprised of stores or service centers, single-site legislation would be a major boon for union organization. Second, the use of Internet organizing could facilitate the organization of service stores or centers that are geographically scattered. Although Internet organizing will become a major tool for labor organizations, unions will not make significant inroads into most service organizations. Unions could make significant gains in one service area—health care services. Health care, now approximately fifteen percent unionized (Bureau of National Affairs 1999b), represents a huge opportunity for union organization. JoAnn Shaw, vice president and chief human resource officer of the University of Chicago Hospitals and Health Systems, says union-organizing activities have increased in number semiannually between 1996 and 1998 from 11.5 percent to 16.6 percent (ASHHRA 1998).

There are some underlying factors that may result in the increase of unionization in the health care industry. First, most health care facilities employ a significant number of employees. Second, many health care companies have continued directive cultures, which cause employees increasing dissatisfaction. Third, unions in this industry have developed some momentum. Employees in a nonunion company may be more susceptible when aware of other organization activities in other health care facilities. In addition, physicians have recently become very interested in unionization. To date approximately 2 percent of the 1.4 million physicians have organized

(Stilwell 1998). While the rationale for physicians to organize is not apparent, the uncertainties of this industry and the new ideological offering of unions appear to be two significant reasons.

The implications and challenges for human resource professionals in health care are enormous. HR personnel should be fully aware that their industry is a hotbed of union-organization activities. It would be prudent to scrutinize company programs, culture, and practices aggressively for causes of employee dissatisfaction in order to anticipate or prevent union-organizing activities. Although unions will not establish significant gains in the service industry as a whole, unions will continue to target all health care workers and will be successful in gaining significant membership.

Transportation

With 1 million union members, and the highest concentration of union members (26.5%) (Bureau of Labor Statistics 1999b), the transportation industry will grow during the next two decades. For example, Julie Showers (1999), managing director-labor relations for Northwest Airlines, states: "Unionization within the airline industry is on the increase, not the decrease. Of the major national carriers, four out of five are heavily unionized." The transportation industry also provides the labor movement with greater visibility. For example, who could not be aware of a strike action against a major carrier? Unlike other unions, organizers of transportation workers will not face significant challenges such as the relocation of jobs or the challenge of organizing scattered groups of workers. Therefore, the transportation industry will provide additional union membership and will establish a stronger and more visible leadership role in the labor movement.

Wholesale and Retail Trade

Like to the service industry, the sales industry has a large number of workers (second to the service industry) and a low union member percentage (5.6%) (Bureau of Labor Statistics 1999b). The challenges for unions are the same in other "scattered employee" groups. In addition, the sales industry has a high concentration of contingent workers, such as students who do not perceive their employment relationship as long term.

Some large retail companies, like some manufacturing companies, will consolidate distribution centers, which could create additional probability of union organization. As discussed for the manufacturing industry, human resource professionals should be diligent in such consolidation efforts in order not to cause unionization. In general, this industry offers unions little opportunity to gain significant membership from the enormous pool of workers.

Construction

The construction industry is a well-recognized bastion of the labor movement. The industry has 1 million union members and a union member concentration of 18.6 percent. There will be some growth in construction jobs, and construction companies will continue to "double breast" or maintain nonunion entities for opportunities of highly competitive bidding (Greenwald 1997). In contrast to other traditional union strongholds, such as manufacturing, unions will experience slight gains in construction union members in the future.

In summary, the future of unions in the private sector presents more challenge than opportunity. The most fertile industry, manufacturing, will decline in union membership. Unions will not be effective at gaining significant numbers of new members in the two huge industries of service and sales. The bright spots for private sector unions will be transportation and health care workers.

Public Sector

In contrast to the private sector, the future of public sector unions is much more optimistic. Public sector union membership is approaching fifty percent of all union membership (Bureau of Labor Statistics 1999b). The unions representing teachers (National Education Association) and government employees (American Federal of State, County, and Municipal Employees) are two of the largest unions in the labor movement. Public sector union membership rate is a lofty 37.2 percent (Bureau of Labor Statistics 1999b). There will be slight growth in the number of government jobs in the future, especially in area of education, although it is apparent that factors such as charter schools and vouchers could result in some erosion of union membership.

Similar to their colleagues in the private sector, public sector employees perceive significant threats from government outsourcing and from privatization. This reduced influence is aggravated by the tendency of public employers to have directive or autocratic cultures. Unions are considered an ally in the minimization of both of these significant threats. In addition, public sector human resource professionals have less influence than their private sector counterparts in the implementation and administration of the programs and processes that directly affect the employees.

Labor legislation is a paramount consideration in the public sector. Consequently, some public sector employees continue to be prohibited from union representation. But legislative limitations will continue to affect only a minority of government employees in the future. Accordingly, private sector unions will gain considerable numbers of members in the future, and public sector unions will dominate the labor movement after experiencing significant growth. The public sector presents few barriers to labor organizations and offers a very large pool of workers attracted to unions.

Conclusion

The future of unions is slightly more favorable than their current state. Unions will continue to represent a substantial number of workers. Based upon this analysis, union membership can be expected to include between 20 and 25 percent of the workforce.

The labor movement will continue to have considerable political clout, and union-sponsored strike actions will continue to have significant impact on the employment climate in this country. Current trends forecast a major shift of power and prominence within the labor movement. Unions representing transportation workers and health workers will rise in influence in the private sector. Public sector employees, including teachers, will comprise the new majority of union membership.

There are several significant implications for human resource professionals, who have a most critical role in providing and nurturing work environments of care, concern, and appreciation for the employees. First, this analysis provides a preview of future union representation in various industries. Each human resource professional should carefully examine the trends and predict the extent to which experience with labor relations will be necessary in their own organizations. Second, and most significant, human resource professionals should have a better understanding of their own individual influence and involvement in the determination of the union status of their particular organizations. Third, human resource professionals should recognize that unionization is not necessarily evidence of deficiencies on the part of either management or the human resource department. Rather, unionization can be systemic or the result of the inclinations and concerns of the workforce. For example, the anxiety and fear of public employees about privatization is not in response to any evidence in their current workplaces. This analysis of historical and current trends is offered to give human resource professionals the opportunity to visualize and shape their futures.

Recommended Actions

- Nurture employee job satisfaction through proper selection, performance feedback, recognition, and job design.
- Provide training and clear expectations for supervisors and managers to ensure fair, respectful, and appropriate treatment of all employees.
- Provide proper communication and equity when implementing employee reductions.
- Provide methods for fostering employee involvement, internal communication, and a sense of personal ownership in the company.

References

Adams, M. "The stream of labor slows to a trickle." HR Magazine, 43(10) (1998): 84–89.

Amber, M. "Union membership numbers." Daily Labor Report. Bureau of National Affairs, Inc. 4 February 1999 [on-line]. Available at http://www.newsstand.k-link.com/nwsstnd.

ASHHRA/OMNI Semi-Annual Labor Activity Report. 1 January–30 June, 1998). 13th report, 1–8.

Bureau of Labor Statistics Census. Employment and Earnings. Bureau of Labor Statistics, Washington, D.C.: U.S. Government Printing Office, January 1984 and January 1998.

Bureau of Labor Statistics. "Union affiliation of employed wage and salary workers by occupation and industry." Bureau of Labor Statistics Table 3, 29 January 1996 [on-line]. Available at http://stats.bls.gov:80/news.release/union2.t03htm.

Bureau of Labor Statistics. "Unions and part-time workers." AFL-CIO, 12 January 1999a [on-line]. Available at http://www.aflcio.org.

Bureau of Labor Statistics. "Union Membership Trends." AFL-CIO, 12 November 1999. [on-line]. Available at http://www.aflcio.org/uniondifference/uniondiff11.htm.

Bureau of National Affairs. Union members by state, 1997. AFL-CIO, 12 January 1999a [on-line]. Available at http:/www.aflcio.org/org/uniondifference/uniondiff16.htm.

Bureau of National Affairs. Union Labor Report: Reference File. BNA. 4 February 1999b [on-line]. Available at http://www.newsstand.k-link.com/nwsstnd.

Department of Labor. "Employment and earnings." AFL-CIO 12 January 1999 [on-line]. Available at http://www.aflcio.org/uniondifference.

Fiorito, J., Lowman, C., and Nelson, F. "The impact of human resource policies on union organizing." *Industrial Relations*, 26(2) (Spring 1987): 113–126.

Foulkes, F. *Personnel Policies in Large Nonunion Companies*. Englewood Cliffs, NJ: Prentice-Hall 1980.

Greenwald, J. "Where the jobs are." *Time*, 149(3) 20 January 1997 [on-line]. Available at http:wysiwyg://cgi.pathfinder.com/time/magazine/1997/dom/97012cover.html.

Holley, W. and Jennings, K. *The Labor Relations Process*. 6th Ed., Orlando, Florida: Harcourt Brace College Publishers, 1997.

Hurd, R. "Contesting the dinosaur image: The labor movement's search for a future." *Labor Studies Journal*, 22(4) (1998):5–42.

Kaufman, B.E. "The future of the labor movement: A look at the fundamentals." *Labor Law Journal*, 48(8) (August 1997):474–484.

Kleiman, L.S. *Human Resource Management*. 8th ed. Minneapolis/St. Paul: West Publishing, 1997.

Mathis, R. and Jackson, J. *Human Resource Management*. 8th ed., Minneapolis/St. Paul: West Publishing, 1997.

Outwater, L. *Daily Labor Report*, Bureau of National Affairs, 9 September 1997, p. 1.

Overman, S. "Unions demand a voice." *HR Magazine* 42(7) (1997)112–118.

Rosenthal, M. "Leadership is critical to resurgence." *Labor Studies Journal* 22(4) (1998):43–46.

Showers, Julie (julie.showers@nwa.com). "Future of unions." E-mail to J. Laumeyer (jim.laumeyer@dot.state.mn.us), 29 January 1999.

Simon, P. Input for the future of unions. In Letter to Jim Laumeyer, 4 January 1999.

Stilwell, E. "Hearing opens on doctor's bid to unionize." Cherry Hill, New Jersey, *Courier-Post*: 5 November 1998, p. 13D.

Wall Street Journal "Women to women." 24 March 1998, p. A1.

Wildavsky, B. "Not happy after NAFTA." *U.S. News and World Report*, 126 (11 January 1999):49.

MEASURING HR'S FUTURE

Raymond B. Weinberg
Research Committee

Folk musician Bob Dylan's hit "The Times They Are A-Changin'" could easily apply to both the last decade and the next for the field of human resource management. Turbulent change presents both challenges and opportunities for human resource practitioners. How HR responds to these challenges and opportunities determines its credibility and ultimately its very survival.

The challenges faced by HR are many. Its critics are widespread, as evidenced by Thomas A. Stewart, who proclaimed in a *Fortune* magazine editorial: "Nestling warm and sleepy in your company like the asp in Cleopatra's bosom is a department whose employees spend 80% of their time on routine administrative tasks. Nearly every function of this department can be done more expertly for less by others. Chances are, its leaders are unable to describe their contribution to value added except in trendy, unquantifiable and wannabe terms—yet, like the serpent unaffected by its own venom, the department frequently dispenses to others advice on how to eliminate work that does not add value" (Stewart 1996, p. 105).

Stewart's criticism, although exaggerated, is not without some degree of merit. HR must be able to measure, in quantifiable terms, the value it adds to organizations. It must learn to forsake HR fads, many of which are cross-dressed as strategic initiatives. It must have an impact and be able to measure that impact on the organization's bottom line. The failure of human resources to measure its contribution has led to its own credibility problem. David Ulrich summed it up well in his appropriately titled article, "Judge Me More by My Future Than by My Past," when he stated, "While the HR as we know it (with images of policy police, regulations and administrative guardians) has passed, a new HR is emerging" (Ulrich 1997b, p. 5). This new HR he proposes must focus on deliverables and impact.

The purpose of this chapter is twofold. First, the chapter examines changes in the workplace that will affect the delivery of HR in the next decade. Robotics, information age technology, and telecommunications will have a profound effect on jobs and organizations. The virtual workplace is close upon us. HR in this workplace may have little resemblance to the HR of today. Second, this chapter will examine measurement of the value added by HR in the next decade's workplace—what will be measured and how it will be measured. Only through measurement can the human resource field regain its credibility.

Measurement—HR's Achilles' Heel

Although the HR function, in one form or another, has been around since before 1900, measurement of HR contributions is a fairly recent development. It wasn't until the mid-1960s that the proponents of a concept called human resource accounting made initial attempts at quantifying the value of human resources (Brummet, Flamholtz, and Pyle 1968). These proponents advocated that the value of human resources be treated as an asset rather than an expense on financial accounting statements. Although not addressing the value of the contribution of the HR function per se, these early pioneers challenged the belief that human resources couldn't be quantified.

Later approaches in measuring the value of the human resource function were primarily activity- and cost-based (Fitz-enz 1984; Cascio 1991). These approaches emphasized cost-effectiveness in justifying HR activities and initiatives.

Today's approaches have focused on measuring the relationship of HR's contribution to the organization. Using objective, quantifiable organizational effectiveness criteria and qualitative measures of HR deliverables, the focus of these approaches has been on drawing a clear line of sight between the quality of HR practices and productivity, sales, earnings per share, profitability, and other measures of an organization's success (Huselid and Becker 1995; Huselid and Becker 1996; Becker et al. 1997; Welbourne and Andrews 1996). Some researchers have even used the list of most admired companies from *Fortune, Inc.*, and *Business Week* in an index (much like the Dow Jones), comparing performance of those firms on the list and comparable firms not on the list, with significant findings (Callette and Hadden 1998). This research justifies the value contributed by HR to the bottom line. Unfortunately, for the typical HR practitioner these measurement methodologies have escaped use. Clearly, the measurement of HR contribution must find its way out of the ivory towers and down to the level of the individual firm if HR is to truly become a business partner.

The New Workplace

The previous decade brought about significant changes to the workplace, creating many challenges for the HR field. The decade gave rise to economic and employment shifts, global competition, organizational restructuring, demographic/ workforce diversity changes, work/family considerations, skill shortages, education and training deficits, and expanding employee rights (Mathis and Jackson 1997). For the most part, these changes were driven in response to pressures from outside of the organization. The challenges that were posed to HR in the 1990s may pale in comparison with the projected challenges over the next ten years.

The next set of challenges will arise from three fundamental transformations in the workplace—the changing nature and structure of jobs, the evolving new relationship between employee and employer, and the new fluid structures that organizations need to be competitive in the dynamic marketplace of the twenty-first century. For the most part, these changes will arise from within the organization. Each of these transformations must be examined in relationship to its impact on HR. With an understanding of the magnitude of these changes, an analysis of how HR's future contribution will be measured can be made.

Jobs

The next decade's workplace will be fundamentally different from today's workplace because jobs will be different. Human resources has long relied on the concept of the job to base many of its activities. Jobs were analyzed by systematically gathering information on their content, requirements, and context. Job analysis and resultant job descriptions were the heart of most HR activities, including recruitment and selection, compensation, training and development, performance appraisal, and legal compliance (Mathis and Jackson 1997). Jobs were highly defined, and human resource activities for the most part derived themselves from the concept of the specialized job.

Both the structure of jobs and the skills required to perform them will undergo a major transformation. Jobs used to be based upon the high-volume industrial model. New information age technology will have a profound effect on these jobs and the very nature of work. In fact, jobs as they are known today may cease to exist in the postindustrial world (Rifkin 1995).

Previously, new technologies have had a trickle-down effect, reducing product costs, increasing consumer demand, and putting more people to work in new information age jobs and industries (Rifkin 1995). In the 1990s, organizations reengineered, productivity grew, profits increased, and all was well for shareholders (Mishel and Bernstein 1992). In all likelihood, the next wave of technological advances will render many jobs obsolete. Premiums will be paid for certain highly skilled jobs in the next decade's workplace. Some analysts have envisioned only three types of jobs in this new era—routine production services, in-person services, and symbolic/analytic services (Reich 1991). Only the skilled symbolic/analytical jobs will be in high demand. HR will have to adjust to these new jobs.

The twenty-first century will also give way to jobs where knowledge and intellectual capabilities are what differentiates one employee from another (Bahrami and Evans 1997). Focus will change from what is done to what one is capable of doing. Instead of compartmentalized, narrow jobs defined by functional or occupational domains, broader, more expansive roles will evolve (Crandall and Wallace 1998). Work is envisioned to move from position-based to person-based systems, where intellectual capital and competencies will constitute the new competitive advantage. As a result, emerging new trends such as virtual workplaces, "anytime/anyplace" work, contingent work, and cyberlinked work will become more commonplace. Human resource practitioners will have to play a pivotal role in adapting HR systems to this new work.

The New Employment Relationship

The euphemism that past behavior is the best predictor of future behavior does not bode well for human resources. The past decade has seen organizations alter the relationship between employer and employee in many ways. Restructuring, reengineering, zero-based staffing, outsourcing, rightsizing, and downsizing have characterized this period. As a result, the commitment of even the most loyal employees has been tested by the psychological contract—an unwritten understanding based upon mutual trust that defines what the employee and the organization expect to give to and receive from each other during their relationship. Before the 1990s the psychological contract was very stable. Employees went to work for employers with reliable expectations for rewards and long-term employment

(Sims 1994). This mutual relationship was based upon employers protecting the interest of employees in return for dedication, hard work, loyalty, and commitment. As organizations' external environments become more chaotic, the psychological contract began to be reshaped.

This altered employment relationship has given way to what has been described as the "new psychological contract" between employees and employers (Rousseau and Geller 1994). As Rousseau and Geller allude, a major function of a human resource manager is to foster an appropriate psychological contract. Human resources officers will be faced with the challenge of redefining expectations under the new psychological contract. They must find means of strengthening the likelihood of mutually satisfying exchange relationship between employees and organizations. The concept of job security, so long sought after by employees, will give way to career security, where competencies and capabilities become the new workplace currency. The workplace that evolves will require flexibility on the part of employees in order to attain this new form of security. As rules of the game change, HR must work harder in making sense out of the new employment relationship.

The New Organization

If the changing nature of jobs and the employment relationship didn't pose enough issues for HR, the organization of the next decade will create a more fluid environment for the delivery of HR services. In the past, organizations were highly structured, with clearly defined boundaries. Organizational success was determined by four factors: size, role clarity, specialization, and control (Ashkenas et al. 1995). The organizational structure determined by these factors tended to be very rigid and departmentalized. Every person had a job and a function, and performance was measured against standards. In the new organization, those historical success factors have been replaced by speed, flexibility, integration, and innovation (Ashkenas et al. 1995). Organizations are moving from fixed boundaries to more fluid boundaries. Lines on the organizational chart have become blurred. The organization of the new workplace will reformulate external, loosen horizontal, and flatten vertical and cross-geographic boundaries. What this means for HR is that its constituency or consumer group will expand far beyond employees. These blurred boundaries will result in former competitors forming strategic alliances and new entities developing that represent the entire length of the value chain (Crandall and Wallace 1998). HR will have a whole new constituency.

These blurred boundaries will spawn the emergence of the virtual organization, one not bounded by visual and physical proximity. Employees will remote-work using telecommunications and technology to fulfill their new roles. HR will also be virtual, with services instantaneous, on demand, and at a place most convenient to its customers. HR administrative functions will be shed, and the focus will be on service and strategic deliverables. Multimedia kiosks, paperless HR, desktop learning, and distance supervision and learning will be commonplace. HR measurement in the new organization will be more difficult.

Measuring Human Resources Value-Added Contribution

Effective human resource practices will be necessary for organizational success and growth. Current research has already verified this relationship (Huselid and Becker 1995). The question becomes what and how do you measure to determine the value-added contribution of HR practices in the workplace of the future. Most economics textbooks define value-added as the incremental addition to profit that results from transformational activity. Numerous terms have been used or misused to describe valued-added, including accountability, return on investment (ROI), effectiveness, worth, impact, cost versus benefit, and bottom line contribution. These terms have in common the emphasis on measuring HR's practices link to tangible business goals. As Ulrich has stated, "These terms focus on results and not activities, deliverables not doables" (Ulrich 1997a, p. 24).

What should be measured? The HR practices of the new workplace have not yet been defined. New practices and tools will be forthcoming. Ulrich says, "These tools will focus on such areas as: global HR (learning to manage HR issues and global competition), culture change (defining tools for crafting and changing corporate culture), technology (adapting HR to the ever-changing information highway), leader of the future (defining the competencies of the future, not past leader) and knowledge transfer (understanding how to generate and generalize knowledge)" (Ulrich 1997b, p. 6).

How can HR measure its value-added for tools and practices not yet defined? Changes in jobs, the employment relationship, and organizations point to measures of HR's value-added contributions in the areas of:

Intellectual capital assessment and investment. This will be the currency of the new workplace. The unmapped and untapped knowledge of an organization will have profound economic impact by creating competitive advantage. HR's role in assessing and developing intellectual capital will affect the bottom line and be a key area for measuring of value-added (Stewart 1997).

Extended value chain enhancement. With new customers beyond the walls of the traditional organization—suppliers, competitors and communities—participating in the value chain, HR will need to collaborate with this extended group in adding value. The measures of HR contribution will go beyond traditional boundaries of the organization to a larger constituency. Broader measures may be needed.

Values stewardship. One way for HR to redefine expectations of its new employment relationship will be through a strengthening of culture. HR must measure the impact of its practices on the shared beliefs and values of the organization, and in turn the impact on the financial goals of the enterprise values redefinition will reshape the psychological contract.

Action learning development. Learning about learning, solving problems in real time will reduce the lag between learning and application and bridge the gap between process and outcomes will have to be measured. (Burke 1995, p. 166).

HR will lead the way in action learning development by calculating translating theory who practice and measuring the return.

Competency-based system application. HR's emphasis on what really affects performance in the organization will help shape the HR tools and practices of the next decade. Competency-based staffing, development, and rewards will become commonplace. Measuring competency development and payoff will be a priority.

The tools and practices of the past give way to these tools and practices of future. These future tools and practices, although still undefined, will have characteristics of adaptability, quick delivery, and measurable impact.

A Word of Caution

In the virtual HR organization of the future, these tools and practices may not rest in the human resource department or function. They very well could be disbursed through line management. The HR department may actually disappear. The question becomes how you measure the contribution of HR practices independent of the HR function (Ulrich 1997b).

Although HR has been accountable for HR practices, in reality the entire organization is responsible for their implementation. HR practices are embodied in organizational practices. They cannot be separated. No matter where HR is performed, effective HR practices will need to be present.

Traditionally, HR measurement and evaluation has had three levels. These are measures of perceived effectiveness (feedback from stakeholders), measures of performance (indicators of HR performance), and measures of return on investment (monetary value of program benefits compared with cost) (Phillips 1996). The movement will be toward return on investment where important business outcomes can be measured—where value-added can be seen.

Conclusion

Measuring HR's contribution has certain payoffs to organizations. Measuring value-added makes good economic sense. Every HR practice should provide a return on investment. Measuring value-added contributions also provides proof of results. By keeping a scorecard of how HR practices affect important organizational outcomes, line management appreciates the value of these practices. By measuring value-added, it encourages the organization to focus on important HR deliverables. It will tie practice outcomes to bottom line contribution. Measuring the value-added HR services increases the function's credibility. By measuring value-added contributions, HR will be viewed not as a staff function, but as a true business partner. "The Times They Are A-Changin'."

Recommended Actions

- Measure HR deliverables rather than activities.

- Calculate ROI for each and every HR program and for the HR function as a whole.
- Change the measurement focus from cost to value.
- In ROI, focus on specifically quantifying the numerator (value) rather than the denominator (cost).
- Build measurement into the design of HR programs in the beginning, rather than after the program has been implemented.

References

Ashkenas, R.; Ulrich, D.; Jick, T.; and Kerr, S. *The Boundaryless Organization*. San Francisco. Jossey-Bass, 1995.

Bahrami, H., and Evans, S. "Human resource leadership in knowledge-based entities: Shaping the context of work." *Human Resource Management* 36(1) (1997):23–28.

Becker, B.; Huselid, M.; Pickus, P.; and Spratt, M. "HR as a source of shareholder value: Research and recommendations." *Human Resource Management* 36(1) (1997):39–47.

Brummet, R.; Flamholtz, E.; and Pyle, W. "Human resource measurement—a challenge for accountants." *Accounting Review* 47(2) (1968):217–227.

Burke, W. "Organizational change: What we know and what we need to know." *Journal of Management Inquiry* 4 (1995):158-171.

Callette, B., and Hadden, R. *Contented Cows Give Better Milk*. Germantown, TN: Saltillo Press, 1998.

Cascio, W. *Costing human resources: The Financial Impact of Behavior in Organizations*. Boston: Kent Publishing, 1991.

Crandall, N. F., and Wallace, M. *Work and Rewards in the Virtual Workplace*. New York: AMACOM, 1998.

Fitz-enz, J. *How to Measure Human Resources Management*. New York: McGraw-Hill, 1984.

Huselid, M., and Becker, B. *High Performance Work Systems and Organizational Performances*. Paper presented at the Academy of Management Annual Conference, Vancouver, British Columbia, 1995.

Huselid, M., and Becker, B. "Methodological issues in cross-sectional and panel estimates of HR-firm performance link." *Industrial Relations* 35(3) (1996):400–422.

Mathis, R., and Jackson, J. *Human Resource Management*. St. Paul: West Publishing Company, 1997.

Mishel, L., and Bernstein, J. *The State of Working America 1992–1993*. Washington, D.C.: Economic Policy Institute, 1992.

Phillips, J. *Accountability in Human Resource Management*. Houston: Gulf Publishing, 1996.

Reich, R. *The Work of Nations*. New York: Random House, 1991.

Rifkin, J. *The End of Work*. New York: G. P. Putnam's Sons, 1995.

Rousseau, D., and Geller, M. "Human resources practices: Administrative contract makers." *Human Resource Management* 33(3), (1994):385–406.

Sims, R. "Human resource management's role in clarifying the new psychological contract." *Human Resource Management* 33(3) (1994):373–382.

Stewart T. *Intellectual Capital: The New Wealth of Organizations*. New York: Doubleday/Currency, 1997.

Stewart, T. "Taking on the last bureaucracy. " *Fortune*, 15 January (1996):105–106, 108.

Ulrich, D. *Human Resource Champions: The Next Agenda for Adding Value and Delivering Results*. Boston: Harvard Business School Press, 1997a.

Ulrich, D. "Judge me more by my future than by my past." *Human Resource Management* 36(1) (1997b):3–8.

Welbourne, T., and Andrews, A. "Predicting performance of initial public offering firms: Should human resource management be in the equation?" *Academy of Management Journal* 39(4) (1996):891–919.

ABOUT THE SOCIETY

Michael R. Losey
Society for Human Resource Management

In reading this book, it becomes obvious that the human resource profession, born less than a century ago, has already undergone enormous change, evolving from essentially a personnel clerk to a senior-level strategic business partner. In the twenty-first century, the human resource profession will truly come of age.

The Society for Human Resource Management has long anticipated these changes in the profession and has endeavored to meet them. For decades the Society has supported functional committees to stay abreast and anticipate changes and issues in such areas as compensation and benefits, labor and employee relations, health, safety and security, training and development, and management practices. Their expertise is reflected in these chapters.

In 1976 the Human Resource Certification Institute (HRCI), an affiliate of the Society, was established to certify the knowledge of those in the human resource profession. To develop the test for certification, the Society and HRCI identified a body of knowledge. That body of knowledge has been growing, and it will continue to expand at exponential rates. Each year HRCI breaks its own records in the number of human resource professionals who take the exams. And, more and more companies are seeking human resource professionals who are certified through the Institute. These companies realize that the human resource profession has a quantifiable body of knowledge that requires study and mastery. They recognize that just as you cannot "sell from an empty wagon" you cannot expect someone to do human resource work "with an empty head." Higher barriers of entrance to the profession are developing.

In discussing the future of the workplace and the human resource profession, the urgency for better education and lifelong learning opportunities for human resource professionals becomes apparent. As the field comes of age, colleges and universities must establish human resource management majors that emphasize strategic business planning in their curricula. The Society has long encouraged the formal study of human resource management and fosters such study through its student and adult education programming.

As previously discussed, the future will require that federal and state laws and regulations change to allow organizations to meet the needs of their workers. The Society has an active governmental affairs department and an award-winning grassroots program to help effect these changes. But these laws and regulations must not be altered without the leadership and input of human resource professionals. Members of Congress and state legislators *must* hear from human resource professionals if these laws are to be amended fairly. It is certainly gratifying to be asked to testify before a federal or state legislative body because it speaks to the importance of the profession in the United States. If the human resource profession is to truly move into its strategic business role, however, human resource professionals must become more active in legislative and regulatory affairs, serving as strategic partners to Congress, state legislators, and regulatory agencies.

Early on, the Society recognized that the world would become a much smaller place in the twenty-first century and that human resource professionals would have to be prepared to cope with increased globalization. So, in 1991, SHRM established the Institute for International Human Resources (IIHR), a division of SHRM that helps educate human resource professionals about the challenges associated with a global economy and to generate solutions. Today, IIHR represents more than 5,300 members in more than forty countries.

SHRM is also a founding member (and currently president) of both the North American Human Resource Management Association (NAHRMA) and the World Federation of Personnel Management Associations (WFPMA). Because of the Society's foresight, it is deeply involved in global issues, with members in more than 100 countries, and therefore it is prepared to assist human resource professionals whose organizations are entering international waters.

ABOUT THE EDITOR

Marc G. Singer is professor of management at Middle Tennessee State University and president of Emadjen Management Consulting. He received his B.B.A. in 1968 from the City College of New York, his M.B.A. in 1971 from Baruch College, and his Ph.D. in 1973 from the University of Tennessee. An active consultant, trainer, and researcher, Dr. Singer specializes in staffing, performance appraisal, and government rules and regulations, particularly as they relate to equal employment opportunity and labor relations. Dr. Singer is widely published in professional journals, he is the author of a textbook on human resource management, and he co-edited the second edition of SHRM's *Effective Human Resource Measurement Techniques* that was sponsored by the SHRM Foundation. From 1997–1999, Dr. Singer served as chair of the SHRM research committee and as a director on the SHRM Foundation Board.

ABOUT THE AUTHORS

Raylana S. Anderson, CEBS, SPHR, a human resource and employee benefits consultant, is the proprietor of Anderson Consulting in Peoria, Illinois. She received her B.A. in 1981 and her M.B.A. in 1988 from Bradley University. In addition to assisting companies in the development of comprehensive employee relations programs and total compensation practices and policies, Ms. Anderson has authored or co-authored several widely used HR compliance guidebooks. Ms. Anderson served as the 1998–1999 chair of the SHRM Compensation and Benefits Committee.

Debbra M. Buerkle, CCP, SPHR, is managing partner with Human Resources & Management Solutions, specializing in employee relations consulting services. She received a B.A. in 1977 from Thiel College and completed master's studies in Applied Communication and Alternative Dispute Resolution at the University of Denver. Actively involved with the SHRM since the mid-1980s, Ms. Buerkle currently serves on the SHRM's Legislative Action Committee. She also has served as Colorado's state legislative affairs director and as the Colorado Springs chapter's legislative affairs liaison.

Robyn Burke, SPHR, is a human resource service delivery executive with Computer Sciences Corporation. She received her B.S. in 1987 and her M.Ed. in 1991 from Vanderbilt University. Over the past several years, Ms. Burke has delivered workshops and training programs on a variety of HR topics; she has designed and implemented performance management, succession planning, and organizational/individual development tools; and she has recently authored a SHRM white paper on managing the careers of high performers. Ms. Burke is a member of the SHRM Human Resource Development Committee.

David F. Bush, is professor of Industrial/Organizational Psychology and coordinator of the graduate program in HRD at Villanova University. He received his B.A. in 1965 from the University of South Florida, his M.A. in 1968 from the University of Wyoming, and his Ph.D. in 1972 from Purdue University. An active researcher and consultant, Dr. Bush has in excess of sixty publications, is the originator of the *Alligator Syndrome*, has developed several assessment instruments, and serves as an editor of the *Journal of Systems Improvement*. An active SHRM member, Dr. Bush has served as president of the Philadelphia regional chapter of the SHRM, and he is currently the professional development chair of the Pennsylvania State Council of the SHRM and a member of the SHRM Workplace Health and Safety Committee.

Cornelia G. Gamlem, SPHR, is corporate manager, employee relations, for Computer Sciences Corporation. She received her B.S. in 1983 from California State University, Sacramento, and her M.A. in 1995 from Marymount University. Ms. Gamlem has extensive experience in the areas of policy-setting and program management, specifically in areas involving equal employment opportunity, affirmative action, employee relations, and workplace diversity. An active writer, Ms. Gamlem has authored several SHRM white papers on topics such as affirmative action, alternative dispute resolution, workplace diversity, and the Family and Medical Leave Act. Ms. Gamlem joined the SHRM Workplace Diversity Committee in 1993 and served as chair in 1997–1999. She served as an at-large member of the 1996 board of directors for the Institute for International Human Resources, and she currently serves as a vice president at-large on the SHRM's 2000 Board of Directors.

Phyllis G. Hartman, SPHR, is director of human resources for Stylette Plastics in Oakdale, Pennsylvania, and an instructor at LaRoche College . She received her B.S. in 1971 from Edinboro State University, and her M.S. in 1990 from LaRoche College. Before her current position, Ms. Hartman worked at SAE International, where she managed staff training and development, and recruiting functions. An active speaker and writer, Ms. Hartman has delivered presentations to various HR associations, and she co-authored a 1994 book chapter on recruitment and staffing for the American Society of Association Executives (ASAE). Ms. Hartman is a former president and member of the board of directors of the Pittsburgh Human Resources Association, she served as the 1998–1999 treasurer of the SHRM Pennsylvania State Council, and she is a member of the SHRM School-to-Work Committee.

Linda S. Johnson is a partner with the law firm of McLane, Graf, Raulerson & Middleton, P.A. She received her B.S. in 1981 from Rivier College and her J.D. in 1984 from Boston University School of Law. In addition to her practice focusing on employment law defense and corporate management, Ms. Johnson has written numerous articles for local publications. Recently she authored "The Employee Handbook: Careful Drafting Makes the Difference Between Having a Sword or a Shield," published in the 1997 edition of the Defense Research Institute's *Employment Law Basics*. Ms. Johnson is a member of the SHRM Employment Committee.

James A. Laumeyer is the director of administration for the Minnesota Department of Transportation, Northeastern Minnesota. He received his B.A. degree in 1973 from Macalester College, and his M.B.A. in 1978 from the University of Minnesota–Duluth. A prolific speaker and writer on topics relating to employer and labor relations, Mr. Laumeyer also serves as an adjunct faculty member at the University of Minnesota–Duluth, the University of Minnesota–Carlson School, and the College of St. Scholastica. Mr. Laumeyer is the past president of the Minnesota Public Employer Labor Relations Association, and the past chair of the SHRM Employee and Labor Relations Committee.

Michael R. Losey, SPHR, CAE, is president and CEO of the SHRM. He received both his B.B.A. and his M.B.A. from the University of Michigan. With more than 40 years of HR experience, Mr. Losey is a frequent spokesperson and writer on HR issues, and he recently co-edited the book *Tomorrow's HR Management*. Mr. Losey currently serves as president of the World Federation of Personnel Management Associations (WFPMA), as president of the North American Human Resource Management Association (NAHRMA), and as a fellow and director of the National Academy of Human Resources (NAHR).

Raymond B. Weinberg, CCP, SPHR, is a principal and senior consultant for the Silverstone Group, Inc. He received his B.S.B.A. in 1973 and his M.B.A. in 1977 from the University of Nebraska at Omaha. Before his current assignment, Mr. Weinberg was human resources director at Father Flanagan's Boys Home, where he was directly responsible for administering all phases of HR for a 1,700-employee youth care organization operating in seventeen cities and eleven states. In addition to his workplace experience, Mr. Weinberg has taught HR-related courses for the past twenty-five years at colleges and universities including Buena Vista University, Metropolitan Community College, and the University of Nebraska at Omaha. Mr. Weinberg is an active member of many professional associations, a member of the SHRM Research Committee, a director on the SHRM Foundation Board, and a past president of the Human Resource Certification Institute. In recognition of his expertise in, and contributions to, the field of HR, Mr. Weinberg was presented with the SHRM 1993 "Award for Professional Excellence."